CONTEXT AND COMMENTARY

Series Editor: ARTHUR POLLARD

Published titles

J. A. V. Chapple
SCIENCE AND LITERATURE IN THE NINETEENTH CENTURY

Pamela Horn
LIFE AND LABOUR IN RURAL ENGLAND, 1760–1850

Elisabeth Jay
FAITH AND DOUBT IN VICTORIAN BRITAIN

Robin Headlam Wells
SHAKESPEARE, POLITICS AND THE STATE

Dominic Hibberd
THE FIRST WORLD WAR

Norman Page
THE THIRTIES IN BRITAIN

Stephen Prickett
ENGLAND AND THE FRENCH REVOLUTION

Alan and Dorothy Shelston
THE INDUSTRIAL CITY, 1820–1870

Forthcoming titles

Roger Richardson
REVOLT AND RESTORATION IN THE SEVENTEENTH CENTURY

Alan Downie
LITERATURE AND POLITICS 1678–1780

THE THIRTIES IN BRITAIN

Norman Page

MACMILLAN

First published 1990

Published by
MACMILLAN EDUCATION LTD
Houndmills, Basingstoke, Hampshire RG21 2XS
and London
Companies and representatives
throughout the world

Typeset by Wessex Typesetters
(Division of The Eastern Press Ltd)
Frome, Somerset

Printed in Hong Kong

British Library Cataloguing in Publication Data
Page, Norman
The Thirties in Britain.—(Context and commentary).
1. English literature, 1900–1945. Influence of
political events, 1920–1940—Critical studies
I. Title II. Series
820'.9'00912
ISBN 0–333–41926–X
ISBN 0–333–41927–8 pbk

Contents

Acknowledgements

The author and publishers wish to thank the following who have kindly given permission for the use of copyright material: Jonathan Cape Ltd and Peters Fraser and Dunlop Ltd on behalf of the Executors of the Estate of C. Day Lewis for extracts from 'Bombers' and 'Newsreel' from *Collected Poems 1954* by C. Day Lewis, and 'Battle of Britain' from *Poems of C. Day Lewis* edited by Ian Parsons, Jonathan Cape and the Hogarth Press; Carcanet Press Ltd for 'A Letter from Aragon' and 'Full Moon at Tierz: Before the Storming of Huesea' from *Collected Writings* by John Cornford, 1986; Ad. Donker (Pty) Ltd and Francisco Campbell Custodio for an extract from 'Flowering Rifle' from *Collected Poems* by Roy Campbell; Faber and Faber Ltd for extracts from 'Autumn Journal', 'Birmingham' and 'The Sunlight on the Garden' from *The Collected Poems of Louis MacNiece*; 'An Elementary School Classroom in a Slum' from *Collected Poems 1928–1953* by Stephen Spender; with Random House, Inc. for extracts from 'Letter to Lord Byron' from *Collected Poems*, 'September 1st, 1939', 'Song for the New Year', 'Spain 1937' and 'In Memory of W. B. Yeats' from *The English Auden: Poems, Essays and Dramatic Writings 1927–1939* by W. H. Auden, edited by Edward Mendelson, copyright © 1977 by Edward Mendelson, William Meredith and Munroe E. Spears, Executors of the Estate of W. H. Auden; John Murray, Publishers, Ltd for an extract from 'Slough' from *Collected Poems* by John Betjeman, 1958; Penguin Books Ltd for 'Farewell Chorus' by David Gascoyne from *Poetry of the Thirties*, edited by Robin Skelton, 1964, copyright © 1964 Robin Skelton.

Every effort has been made to trace all the copyright holders, but if any have been inadvertently overlooked the publishers will be pleased to make the necessary arrangements at the first opportunity.

List of Plates

Editor's Preface

J.H. Plumb has said that 'the aim of (the historian) is to understand men both as individuals and in their social relationships in time. "Social" embraces all of man's activities – economic, religious, political, artistic, legal, military, scientific – everything, indeed, that affects the life of mankind.' Literature is itself similarly comprehensive. From Terence onwards writers have embraced his dictum that all things human are their concern.

It is the aim of this series to trace the interweavings of history and literature, to show by judicious quotation and commentary how those actually working within the various fields of human activity influenced and were influenced by those who were writing the novels, poems and plays within the several periods. An attempt has been made to show the special contribution that such writers make to the understanding of their times by virtue of their peculiar imaginative 'feel' for their subjects and the intensely personal angle from which they observe the historical phenomena that provide their inspiration and come within their creative vision. In its turn the historical evidence, besides and beyond its intrinsic importance, serves to 'place' the imaginative testimony of the writers.

The authors of the several volumes in this series have sought to intermingle history and literature in the conviction that the study of each is enhanced thereby. They have been free to adopt their own approach within the broad general pattern of the series. The topics themselves have sometimes also a particular slant and emphasis. Commentary, for instance, has had to be more detailed in some cases than in others. All the contributors to the series are at one, however, in the belief (at a time when some critics would not only divorce texts from their periods but even from their authors) that literature is the creation of actual men and women, actually living in an identifable set of historical circumstances, themselves both the creatures and the creators of their times.

ARTHUR POLLARD

Introduction

The perceived shape of history has from earliest times been fashioned by reigns and wars and natural disasters; but the growing historical self-consciousness of the nineteenth century brought an awareness of centuries and decades, the more or less arbitrary numerical units of time, as imposing their own patterns or grids on the flux of events. A new habit develops in the Victorian period of speaking of 'the present century' or 'the century in which we live'. In a way it would be difficult to match in earlier periods, writers show their consciousness of their own age in relation to the past: Carlyle titles a book *Past and Present*, Trollope calls one of his novels *The Way We Live Now*, Dickens calls one of his *Hard Times, for These Times* and begins another, *Our Mutual Friend*, with the phrase 'In these times of ours', while an important Victorian journal was titled *The Nineteenth Century*. And because they were aware of the unprecedented speed of change the Victorians came to think not only of centuries but of decades and even of years as having their own distinctive characteristics: the Nineties were different from other decades, and 1851 had its prominent mid-century position reinforced by the Great Exhibition.

In our own century the habit has persisted and grown, so that virtually every decade – the Twenties, for instance, or the Sixties – has by general consent or for journalistic convenience been assigned its own distinguishing features. A decade is of course a man-made and not a natural division of time, and there is no inherent reason why, say, the period 1930–39 should constitute a more integral phase of history than, say, 1925–35 or 1937–47 (or, for that matter, 1926–38 or 1936–51). As it happens, though, there are good reasons, or at least reasons solider than popular folklore or journalistic myth, for speaking of the Thirties. Between the end of the First World War on 11 November 1918 and the beginning of the Second World War on 3 September 1939 is a period of less than 21 years, or almost exactly two decades; and it seems natural, if not inevitable, to think of them as 'the Twenties' and 'the Thirties'.

Moreover, history sometimes conspires in an odd way to encourage our tendency to believe that centuries and decades are something more than arbitrary divisions of time. Queen Victoria, whose reign dominates nineteenth-century Britain, died in the first month of the new century; the short reign of her son Edward VII lasted almost exactly a decade. A.J.P. Taylor, a historian of twentieth-century England, has written:

> September 1931 marked the watershed of English history between the wars. Though any division of time above a year is arbitrary, arising only from our habit of counting with arabic numerals by ten, decades take on a character of their own. What was at first merely a convenience for historians is accepted as a reality by ordinary men when they become more literate and judge the world more from books and newspapers than from their own experience. The 'twenties' and the 'thirties' were felt to be distinct periods even at the time, and September 1931 drew the line between them. The break can be defined in many ways. The end of the gold standard was the most obvious and the most immediate. Until 21 September 1931 men were hoping somehow to restore the self-operating economy which had existed, or was supposed to have existed, before 1914. After that day, they had to face conscious direction at any rate so far as money was concerned.
>
> By what was probably a coincidence, exactly the same sort of change took place in international affairs at exactly the same time. Here, too, British policy in the nineteen-twenties had striven to erase the effects and even the memory of the World war. Peace was regarded as the natural rule, its operation impeded only by foolish suspicions. Even those who saw some good in the settlement of 1919 hoped that frontiers, and with them international resentments, would 'fade away'. On 10 September 1931 Viscount Cecil, speaking for the British government, told the League of Nations

> Assembly: 'there has scarcely been a period in the world's history when war seems less likely than it does at present'. A week later, on 18 September, Japanese troops moved into Manchuria, which was nominally under the suzerainty of China.
>
> *English History 1914–1945* (Penguin edn, 1970) pp.374–5.

A small, pedantic, but not insignificant issue needs to be disposed of at this stage. Strictly speaking, the decade of the Thirties began on 1 January 1931 and continued until 31 December 1940, just as some will (quite rightly) insist that the twentieth century began in January 1901. But common practice prefers to regard the Thirties as running from 1930 to 1939 inclusive (just as, no doubt, the arrival of the 21st century will be celebrated at the end of 1999); and for the purposes of this book common practice will be followed.

Seen in these terms, the fourth decade of the twentieth century is not merely an arbitrary slice of history but assumes a shape moulded by actual events. For many of its writers, indeed, it was (as Robin Skelton reminds us in his introduction to *Poetry of the Thirties*) a highly self-conscious decade – conscious of its own distinctive identity *as* a decade. Another, less chronologically precise, term that recurs both in the period and in discussions of the period is 'generation', and this seems to point to the same self-consciousness, the same awareness of being at a unique point in history. Samuel Hynes titles his important study of the Thirties *The Auden Generation*, and Auden himself writes in *Letters from Iceland* (1937) of the 'generation/ That grew up with their fathers at the War' (p.205).

A natural terminus to the decade is the outbreak of war a little less than four months before its end as defined above. But if it was, in common parlance, a period of 'peace', the peace was of a deeply and increasingly troubled kind. Beginning in economic crisis, the decade continued in social hardship and protest at home and war abroad, and drew to an end in the spectre of European war assuming a more distinct and unmistakable shape. This volume will be mainly concerned with events in Britain and their reflection in the work of British writers; but it is important to remember that the Great Depression with which the decade opened was a worldwide phenomenon, just as the conflict in which it ended was a world war.

Though the Thirties have a character that is not entirely imposed by mythmakers, however, it goes without saying that no decade can be a self-contained unit of history; and, more generally, we need to be on our guard against the temptation to generalise, categorise and over-simplify when confronted by the events and the cultural products of a rich and multifarious period. A.T. Tolley has warned against the habit of regarding the Thirties as other than intimately related to the periods that preceded and followed:

> The nineteen-thirties belong to the mythology of our time as well as to its history. In retrospect they seem startlingly encapsulated: they begin with the Wall Street crash in 1929 and end with the invasion of Poland in 1939. They are the "hungry" thirties; the era of appeasement: before, there was unthinking prosperity; afterwards, war. In fact the thirties were not so dramatic in their inception or conclusion. The economic difficulties of parts of Great Britain had their origins in the twenties and were manifest in the General Strike of 1926; while, at the end of the period, there is a gradual change after the Munich agreement in 1938, though the event that truly closes the era is the fall of France in 1940.
>
> The thirties were not as homogeneous as they appear in popular memory. What images does the period evoke? The hunger marches; the Nuremberg rallies; frontiers disappearing; unemployed miners scrambling for coal on dirt tips? Or Baldwin,* with his pipe, cannily moralising to the public during the abdication crisis of 1936, or making Mary Webb's fortune by publicly mentioning her novels? George V was con-

*Stanley Baldwin (1867–1947) was Prime Minister in the Conservative governments of 1923–4 and 1924–9, and also led the National Government in 1935–7.

> cerned most, when a Labour government came into power, about whether proper protocol would continue to be observed in dress for visits to the palace. Both outwardly and inwardly, the thirties had an element of the Victorian as well as an element of the progressive.
>
> *The Poetry of the Thirties* (1975), p.23.

This is a salutary warning, and it should be borne in mind that, while the most passionate and insistent literary voices of the period were nearly all those of young writers, many of those who lived – and voted – during the period had, like George V and Stanley Baldwin, passed their formative years in the reign of Queen Victoria.

As already suggested, memories of the Great War were still fresh in the Thirties: when that decade opened, the war was itself little more than a decade in the past. In *The Great War and Modern Memory* (1975) Paul Fussell has powerfully argued that the Great War, in so many respects unprecedented in human history, radically and permanently altered human perceptions and attitudes. Tolley has reminded us that, for those living in the Thirties, memories of the war had a profound influence on the present:

> No event in the period itself had as great an influence on the course of events as did the memory of the Great War. War was to be avoided at all costs; so war must never be resorted to to settle international differences. These attitudes were associated with policies of pacificism and disarmament. On the other hand, Germany had started the Great War, and German rearmament under Hitler threatened renewed war. It could only be stopped by firm action; and firm action demanded strength, which in turn demanded rearmament. . . .
>
> These attitudes must be borne in mind in reviewing the familiar pattern of the main international events of the decade that seem so decidedly to presage war. In January, 1933, Hitler became Chancellor of Germany. In March the Nazis assumed dictatorial powers, and Germany left the League of Nations in October. Italy

> attacked Abyssinia in October, 1935, completing the conquest in May, 1936. In the meantime, Germany had remilitarised the Rhineland in March; and in July right-wing elements of the army in Spain revolted to begin the Spanish Civil War. The Sino-Japanese conflict was renewed in July, 1937, with the taking of Peking, Nanking and Shanghai. Germany occupied Austria in March, 1938, and followed this with the annexation of the Sudetan areas of Czechoslovakia under an agreement reached with Britain, France and Italy at Munich in September. The remainder of Czechoslovakia was taken over in March, 1939, the month in which the fascists achieved victory in the Spanish Civil War. Germany and the Soviet Union signed a pact of non-aggression in August; and in September Germany invaded Poland and the Second World War began.
>
> Op. cit., pp.23–4.

Again, though, we must be on our guard against over-simplifying the infinitely complex public and private histories of a whole period for our own mental convenience; and Tolley goes on to argue that although 'in retrospect these events seem to lead inexorably towards war', yet 'various things contributed to the pattern not being generally recognised'; and moreover that in any case 'War and the inevitability of war was not the main preoccupation of most people in Great Britain throughout the decade' (pp.24–5). Perhaps this last statement savours of tautology or truism, for in any age the majority of people are primarily concerned with making a living, bringing up their families, getting on with their friends and neighbours, pursuing their hobbies or dreams. And during the Thirties there was plenty for the ordinary man or woman to worry about apart from the international situation.

To look back at a decade is a very different matter from living through it: in the history books the voices of statesmen and politicians tend to drown the rest, and the voices of the poets and novelists and essayists, however eloquent and unforgettable, may not be wholly representative. As Tolley suggests, while it is easy with hindsight to think of the Second World War as both inevitable and casting a long shadow backwards, that was not a universally or even perhaps a very widely held conviction at the time. The League of Nations, an international organisation founded in 1920 with its headquarters at Geneva and not formally dissolved until 1946, was initially the object of high hopes as a means of keeping the peace. During the Thirties, however, it steadily lost credibility as some of its members withdrew (Germany and Japan in 1933, Italy in 1937) and as the sanctions or boycotts that it urged against aggressors proved ineffective. Disarmament campaigns, non-intervention during the Spanish Civil War, the appeasement of Hitler, all failed to avert the coming struggle. Yet it was only natural at the time for many, including some in positions of power and authority, to hope and believe that the worst would not happen. Nearer home Britain's share in the world-wide slump, mass unemployment and problems of housing, diet and health made this a harsh period to live through for millions of people, especially in the industrial regions.

In this volume we shall look at some of the literary and other evidence that helps to create for us a picture of the decade. But again we should be wary of generalisations. 'If the 1920s were a decade when writers tended to turn away in fatigue, boredom, and disgust from everyday problems of social living and political choice,' writes G.S. Fraser, 'the 1930s forced the writer's attention back on the intractable public world around him' (*The Modern Writer and his World*, 1964, p.131); and Fraser's chapter on the period is titled 'The "Serious" 1930s'. Clearly, however, he is not referring to 'writers' but to *some* writers – a group singled out for prominence to support a particular view of the age; and it might also be urged that what he has in mind are *young* writers. 'We grew up under the shadow of war' declared the poet and anthologist Michael Roberts (1902–48) in his preface to *New Country* (1933). But there were writers active in the decade who had *not* grown up under the shadow of war, either because they were too old or because they were too young. 'The Auden generation' is a phrase that commemorates one of the most arresting new voices of the epoch; but it hardly serves as a comprehensive label for a period that, like any other, included writers who were in mid-career and some who had survived from earlier epochs, as well as those who had only recently made their appearance.

Kipling and Yeats, for instance, had begun their careers in the nineteenth century but wrote their last and not inconsiderable works in the Thirties; both were dead before the decade ended. The deaths of other notable authors are listed in the chronology at the end of this volume; some, like D.H. Lawrence, died prematurely, but many – Arthur Conan Doyle, J.M. Barrie, John Galsworthy, G.K. Chesterton, A.E. Housman, and others – seem like improbable survivors from a vanished age and remind us how much the literary world, and the larger world, had changed during their lifetimes. A few long-lived authors such as E.M. Forster, G.B. Shaw and H.G. Wells, who had grown up in the Victorian age, survived the decade and produced significant work in the course of it. Like a family or a community, the literary scene involved several generations co-existing.

Nevertheless, it remains true that most (though not all) of the strongest responses to the age came from younger writers: to be more precise, those who had been born during the opening years of the century, had been too young to fight in the Great War, and were in their twenties at the opening of the decade that is our concern. These include Evelyn Waugh (b.1903), George Orwell (b.1903), Graham Greene (b.1904), Christopher Isherwood (b.1904), Cecil Day Lewis (b.1904), Anthony Powell (b.1905), Louis MacNeice (b.1907) and Stephen Spender (b.1909), all of whom will be summoned as witnesses in the chapters that follow and some of whom saw themselves quite explicitly as spokesmen for their age. This was the generation that, in Michael Roberts' phrase, had grown up 'under the shadow of war'; and Samuel Hynes juxtaposes this quotation with one from a poem by Stephen Spender in which an almost identical phrase is used in a different connection:

> Who live under the shadow of a war,
> What can I do that matters?

Hynes comments:

> The metaphor is the same, but the shadows are different, cast by different wars; it is one of the peculiar burdens of the 'thirties generation that it moved into the shadow of the coming world war before the shadow of the past war had faded.
>
> *The Auden Generation* (1976), p.38.

As we shall see, individuals responded in different ways to this sense of catastrophe behind them and menace ahead, but it is true that almost any activity at that time could be coloured directly or indirectly by an awareness of war. Auden and MacNeice's *Letters from Iceland* makes the point:

> Though writing in a 'holiday' spirit, its authors were all the time conscious of a threatening horizon to their picnic – world-wide unemployment, Hitler growing every day more powerful and a world-war more inevitable. Indeed, the prologue to that war, the Spanish Civil War, broke out while we were there [i.e., in Iceland].
>
> Preface to revised edition of *Letters from Iceland* (1967), p.8; the book originally appeared in 1937.

As the left-wing journalist Kingsley Martin observes in his autobiographical volume *Father Figures* (1966), 'The confusion and perplexity of that time are now hard to communicate' (p.203).

We should remember, however, that international crises and national hardships made up only part of the daily texture of experience for those who lived through the decade, and it may be useful to recall some of the largely non-political factors that made the decade a period of rapid change, not always for the worse. The population of Great Britain increased during the Thirties from 44 795 357 (1931) to 46 560 000 (1939) though the birth rate itself actually declined, partly in continuation of a trend that had begun in the 1870s, but also in response to the economic hardships of the early

Thirties. The increase was partly accounted for by a rise in immigration, including many who fled from Hitler's Germany.

The Welfare State was still a planners' dream and the National Health Service had not yet come into existence to provide medical and hospital care for all who needed it. The school leaving age was 14: plans to raise it to 15 on 1 September 1939 were abandoned on account of the War. Most adolescents attended elementary schools (only one in five in 1931 was receiving secondary education); and the universities were still largely monopolised by the well-to-do (only 6 per cent of the pupils in state secondary schools went on to a university education). In the re-housing of slum-dwellers, however, real progress was made, and despite the slump the building industry flourished during these years: on 1 May 1939 the four millionth house to be built in Britain since the end of the Great War was completed. Housing Acts in 1930, 1933 and 1935 went a considerable way towards solving the problems of overcrowding and sub-standard housing that were a legacy from the Victorian age. Seebohm Rowntree's *Poverty and Progress* (1941) shows in detail how much things had improved during the first third of the twentieth century in one English city, York: whereas in 1900 26 per cent of the inhabitants lived in slum dwellings, by 1936 the proportion had dropped below 12 per cent. But that latter figure reminds us that there was still a considerable way to go; and of the homes deemed acceptable many lacked what would nowadays be regarded as basic amenities (only one-third of homes had bathrooms, for instance). In 1937 there were only 300 domestic refrigerators in the whole of Britain.

In many ways life was becoming more pleasurable. The new popular media of the radio and the talking picture were enjoyed by millions. In 1930 3 092 000 wireless licences were taken out, implying an audience of perhaps four or five times that number. It was the age of the popular entertainer who often belonged to a tradition derived from the music-hall and whose name, thanks to broadcasting, now became a household word; also of famous dance-bands such as those of Henry Hall and Joe Loss. On a more august level, George V in 1932 inaugurated the tradition, still current, of the monarch addressing the nation by its fireside on the afternoon of Christmas Day.

During the Thirties the cinema made great strides as a medium of popular entertainment. The coming of the talkies at the end of the previous decade had given an impetus to the film-making industry and to the builders of cinemas. In 1929 eight sound films had been made; three years later the number was 127; and this produced a remarkable growth in the number of cinemas, which were now to be found in even the smaller towns. The well-known Odeon circuit was formed in 1933. Twenty million tickets a week were sold, and it was estimated that a quarter of the population went to 'the pictures' twice a week or more, to enjoy a substantial programme of entertainment that might include two full-length feature films as well as cartoons or 'shorts' and 'the news'. Programmes were dominated by the products of Hollywood, where the star system was in its heyday: representative films of the period were the early thrillers of Alfred Hitchcock such as *The Thirty-Nine Steps*, Chaplin's *City Lights* and *Modern Times* (the latter a 1936 satire on the world of mass production), Boris Karloff in *Frankenstein*, and (a British product for once) Gracie Fields, the Lancashire mill-girl who became an enormously popular star, in *Sally in Our Alley*, as well as, more exotically, Greta Garbo in *Anna Karenina* and *Camille*. Shirley Temple achieved world-wide fame as a child star, and Tarzan became a popular hero. At the end of the decade *Gone with the Wind*, an immensely long Technicolour epic of the American Civil War, broke records in several directions.

Another popular pastime that flourished was spectator sports. It was the age of legendary cricketers such as Donald Bradman (425 not out in the 1930–31 season) and Len Hutton; also of the huge popularity of Association football (royal attendance at the Cup Final was another tradition established by George V). Football pools, the working man's equivalent of a flutter on the Stock Exchange, became a regular habit for millions during this period: by 1936, for instance, between five and seven million people sent in a weekly entry in the hope of suddenly becoming rich, or at least of enjoying a modest windfall.

Popular newspapers conducted a mass circulation war and vied with each other to shower their subscribers with gifts or bribes: many a working-class home possessed a set of Dickens acquired in this way. *Picture Post*, a popular illustrated magazine, had a wide circulation and provided a remarkable pictorial record of topical events until it expired in 1958 – killed, one presumes, by television. The hunger for images was satisfied at a juvenile level by 'comics', and few children did not peruse *Dandy, Beano, Film Fun* or one of the other favourites with their own casts of folk-heroes. (In this pre-television age the young were also catered for by Saturday morning cinema shows, which attracted large and exuberant audiences.) At the other end of the spectrum the left-wing weekly *New Statesman*, formed by the amalgamation of two existing journals, appeared in 1931 and throughout these years provided vigorous commentary on political and social issues, its editor, Kingsley Martin, remaining in office until 1960. The Cambridge journal *Scrutiny*, edited by F.R. Leavis, was founded in 1932 and offered radical re-examinations of accepted literary judgements. The public libraries were well patronised by people of all ages; it was among other things the great age of the English detective story. Penguin Books, founded by Allen Lane in the middle of the decade, made full-length books available for a few pence and inaugurated the paperback revolution. Among the first titles to be published in 1936 were novels by authors as diverse as Agatha Christie and Ernest Hemingway. The non-fiction companion-series, Pelican Books, followed in 1937.

Travel over both short and long distances was becoming easier. Trams, the democratic mode of travel popular until the late twenties, were increasingly replaced by buses. Private car ownership expanded dramatically: in 1920 there were fewer than 200 000 vehicles registered, but the number climbed to more than a million by 1930 and to nearly two million by the end of the decade. (Driving tests and the speed limit of 30 m.p.h. in built-up areas were introduced in 1934.) It was also the age of the ocean liner: the *Queen Mary* was launched in 1934, the *Queen Elizabeth* in 1938, and both provided luxurious and rapid transatlantic travel. It was only in 1939 that commercial flights between Europe and the USA began, and only much later that they became generally popular.

More people were taking holidays. The Holidays with Pay Act of 1938 meant that millions were for the first time able to take an annual holiday. Two years earlier the first commercial holiday camp had been established at Skegness in Lincolnshire; and 'Butlin's' soon became a byword for modestly priced seaside holidays for the working classes. By the end of the decade there were about a hundred such camps. For the more energetic and the less gregarious the Youth Hostels Association had been founded in 1930, and nearly 300 hostels had opened before war put an end to most holidays and much travelling.

Thanks to the popularity of the hire-purchase system, furnishings and appliances were more readily available. The production of vacuum cleaners, for instance, increased during the first half of the decade from less than forty thousand to over four hundred thousand per year. Many of the appurtenances of everyday life that are now commonplace – including (to cite a few random examples from hundreds of possible instances) penicillin, magnetic tape, the contraceptive pill, colour television, and long-playing records – were still in the future, as were such now-familiar phenomena as organ transplants, supersonic flights, and the atomic bomb; but the Thirties saw the advent of numerous inventions that in lesser or greater ways revolutionised daily life then or a little later. Some examples are nylon stockings, the ballpoint pen (in popular usage commemorating one of its inventors, Georg Biro), DDT, polythene, the jet engine and the discovery of Vitamin D.

While, therefore, this book will inevitably be concerned for the most part with the major public events and issues of the time, it is as well to remember that for those who lived through the Thirties these events and issues were foregrounded by other changes in their lives. For a child growing up in the Thirties (as I did myself) momentous happenings on the national or international stage could manifest themselves at a popular and far from solemn level: just as the increase in smoking during the period could make itself felt to a child not as a set of statistics but through the craze for collecting the cigarette cards given away with each packet by competing manufacturers, so the abdication crisis could be expressed through a parody of a Christmas carol –

> Hark! the herald angels sing,
> Mrs. Simpson's pinched our king. . .

– and the darkness that fell over Europe in 1939 could be expressed through the jaunty or sentimental popular songs of the day (two favourites of that year were 'We'll hang out the washing on the Siegfried Line' and 'The last time I saw Paris'). I recall, too, an unauthorised topical version of a song that was on everyone's lips in 1938, 'Whistle while you work', from Walt Disney's popular *Snow White and the Seven Dwarfs*:

> Whistle while you work,
> Mussolini made a shirt,
> Hitler wore it, Chamberlain tore it,
> Whistle while you work. . . .

By such means was the Munich crisis of 1938 absorbed, with scant regard for factual precision, into the popular consciousness.

This volume will draw its evidence from less demotic, more canonical or academic texts; but it seems worth stressing what ought to be obvious, that poets and novelists, essayists and propagandists, took as their subject matter themes that were woven into the experience of millions who never wrote or even read works aspiring to literary status. There will be no harm in giving prominence to certain voices provided we remember that any attempt to deal briefly with a period as complex and crucial as the Thirties must resort to over-simplifications – which is another way of saying distortions and partial truths. Literary historians, anxious to bring order to the chaotic scene and to discern 'major influences' and 'significant trends', have sometimes suggested that the period has, like a well-made novel or play, a clearly structured 'plot'; but Samuel Hynes wisely concludes *The Auden Generation* by questioning some of the assumptions that have been widely held – 'a set of assumptions about the 'thirties and the younger writers of that decade that remain the commonplace of literary history'. He adds:

> That set will include the following propositions:
>
> The 'thirties may be treated critically as a single historical entity with a fixed and definable character;
>
> It was a period marked by intellectual error, false hopes, delusion, and dishonesty;
>
> The fact that it ended in war may therefore be considered as a deserved destiny, a just punishment for moral failure;
>
> Its writers were all of necessity politically motivated;
>
> Their efforts to make literature a mode of action failed, and their writing shared in that failure.
>
> These are all arguable propositions, but none is entirely true; they are the constituents of a myth by which a complex, confused, often contradictory time has been simplified in order that it might be comprehended. There is no way of reducing the period (or any historical period for that matter) to order *except* by such simplifications, and of course all history is myth-making in this sense. But some myths come closer to reality than others, incorporate more of the disorderly facts in their orders; and all historical myths must be re-examined from time to time, and a new effort made to make them stretch farther, to assimilate more, and to approach more nearly to the complexity of truth.
>
> Op. cit., p.393.

Hynes's final quotation is George Orwell's summing up in 1940 of the decade that had just ended. 'What a decade!' Orwell wrote:

> A riot of appalling folly that suddenly becomes a nightmare, a scenic railway ending in a torture-chamber. It starts off in the hangover of the 'enlightened' post-war age, with Ramsay MacDonald soft-soaping into the microphone and the League of Nations flapping vague wings in the background, and it ends

> up with twenty thousand bombing planes darkening the sky and Himmler's masked executioner whacking women's heads off on a block borrowed from the Nuremberg museum. In between are the politics of the umbrella and the hand-grenade. The National Government coming in to 'save the pound', MacDonald fading out like the Cheshire Cat, Baldwin winning an election on the disarmament ticket in order to rearm (and then failing to rearm), the June purge, the Russian purges, the glutinous humbug of the abdication, the ideological mix-up of the Spanish war, Communists waving Union Jacks, Conservative MPs cheering the news that British ships have been bombed, the Pope blessing Franco, Anglican dignitaries beaming at the wrecked churches of Barcelona, Chamberlain stepping out of his Munich aeroplane with a misquotation from Shakespeare, Lord Rothermere acclaiming Hitler as 'a great gentleman', the London air-raid syrens blowing a false alarm as the first bombs drop on Warsaw.*
>
> 'The Limit to Pessimism', *New English Weekly*, 25 April 1940, p.5.

But, as Hynes reminds us, Orwell's summary is itself 'part of the Myth', and a different summary might be made that would convey a different impression. In the chapters that follow, as we examine some of the major issues and anxieties of the age, a variety of viewpoints will be presented; but, while each spokesman appears as one living through the age and therefore speaking for his own generation and his own time, each is speaking from a point of view that is necessarily

*Some of the allusions that were instantly familiar to Orwell's readers may now need elucidation. Ramsay MacDonald (1866–1937) led the first Labour government in 1924 and was Prime Minister twice again (Labour government of 1929–31; National Government of 1931–5). In Baldwin's National Government (1935–7) he was Lord President. Heinrich Himmler (1900–45) was Hitler's chief of police. General Francisco Franco (1892–1975) was a Spanish military dictator who overthrew the elected government with Nazi and Fascist support. Neville Chamberlain (1869–1940), Conservative Prime Minister 1937–40, was associated with the policy of appeasement. Viscount Rothermere (1868–1940) was a newspaper magnate who founded the mass-circulation *Daily Mirror* and *Sunday Pictorial* and also controlled other leading newspapers.

individual and partial. The value of bringing together these voices as a chorus is that a number of viewpoints may give a less incomplete idea of a truth that in the nature of things can never be wholly recaptured.

1 The Great Depression: Unemployment and Poverty

In the autumn of 1933 the popular novelist J.B. Priestley (1894–1984) set out on a journey that took him throughout most of the length and breadth of England, from Southampton and Bristol to Lancashire and Tyneside; and early in the following year he published an account of his travels. *English Journey* begins in the south, and its tone is at first relaxed and good-humoured. When he reaches the Black Country, however, Priestley's manner becomes less genial: of one street in West Bromwich, for instance, he writes:

> I have never seen such a picture of grimy desolation as that street offered me. If you put it, brick for brick, into a novel, people would not accept it, would condemn you as a caricaturist and talk about Dickens.

Nearby, he adds, there stands 'the last dairy farm in the district. . . surrounded for miles by the grim paraphernalia of industrialism'.

When he arrives in Lancashire, Priestley finds not only ugly towns and a landscape despoiled by the 'dark satanic mills' of the Industrial Revolution but human misery, the result of unemployment and poverty brought about by the decline of the cotton trade. And when he crosses the Pennines and explores the north-east, he finds that, although he had expected conditions to be bad there, they are 'far worse than anything I imagined':

> It far outran any grim expectations of mine. My guide-book devotes one short sentence to Jarrow: "A busy town (35,590 inhabitants), has large ironworks and shipbuilding yards." It is time this was amended

> into "an idle and ruined town (35,590 inhabitants, wondering what is to become of them), had large ironworks and can still show what is left of shipbuilding yards." The Venerable Bede spent part of his life in this neighbourhood. He would be astonished at the progress it has made since his time, when the river ran, a clear stream, through a green valley. There is no escape anywhere in Jarrow from its prevailing misery, for it is entirely a working-class town. One little street may be rather more wretched than another, but to the outsider they all look alike. One out of every two shops appeared to be permanently closed. Wherever we went there were men hanging about, not scores of them but hundreds and thousands of them. The whole town looked as if it had entered a perpetual penniless bleak Sabbath. The men wore the drawn masks of prisoners of war.
>
> *English Journey* (1934), pp.313–14.

Nor is Jarrow unique, for things are no better in the neighbouring town of Hebburn:

> Hebburn is another completely working-class town. It is built on the same mean proletarian scale as Jarrow. It appeared to be even poorer than its neighbour. You felt that there was nothing in the whole place worth a five-pound note. It looked as much like an ordinary town of that size as a dust-bin looks like a drawing-room. Here again, idle men – and not unemployable casual labourers but skilled men – hung about the streets, waiting for Doomsday. Nothing, it seemed, would ever happen here again.
>
> Ibid. p.314.

Particularly vivid is Priestley's description of Hebburn's once-thriving but now derelict shipyard:

> . . . a fantastic wilderness of decaying sheds, strange mounds and pits, rusted iron, old concrete and new

> grass. Both my companions knew about this yard, which had been a spectacular failure in which over a million of money had been lost. . . . As we came to the sullen water-front, we could hear the noise of the electric riveting from the few yards working across the river; but both of them agreed that it seemed quiet now compared with the deafening din of the riveters in the old days. There was one ship in the yards now where there used to be twenty. Down the Tyne we could see the idle ships lying up, a melancholy and familiar sight now in every estuary round the coast. There is hardly anything that brings you more sharply into line with the idiotic muddle of our times than the spectacle of these fine big steamers rusting away in rows.
>
> Ibid. p.316.

Many of the points made by Priestley are echoed in another book published three years later, George Orwell's *The Road to Wigan Pier*; Valentine Cunningham has suggested, indeed, that the earlier book was an important influence on the later one. In January 1936, Orwell (pseudonym of Eric Blair, 1903–50) was commissioned by the left-wing publisher Victor Gollancz to write a book about conditions among the unemployed in the north of England. Orwell is a major spokesman for the period who will often be referred to in this study; and his biographer, Bernard Crick, has argued that his journey to Lancashire was 'crucial' in his development as a thinker and writer. As Crick relates, Orwell spent two months in the north and had finished his book before the end of the year, so that his vivid documentary account refers to working-class life in the town of Wigan in 1936. Like Priestley, he travelled first through the Black Country:

> . . . he took a train to Coventry, but then for five days he made his way north to Manchester, partly on foot and partly on buses, through Birmingham and Stourbridge to Macclesfield, through the 'Black Country': in other words, passing through some

of the grimmest urban spoil of the first industrial revolution just to see what he could see.

George Orwell: A Life (Penguin edn, 1982) p.280.

He stayed in cheap hotels and common lodging houses. At the suggestion of a friend who was a trade union official, Orwell went to Wigan, where unemployment was high, and lived in lodgings in a working-class home in order to see conditions at first hand. Although he was in Wigan for only a few weeks before moving on to Yorkshire, his portrayal of the daily life of the unemployed miners and factory-workers has become classic.

Orwell's method is to combine the recording of facts, including official statistics, with a sharp, unsentimental rendering of the human realities behind the facts and figures. Thus, on the rate of unemployment, he writes:

> When you see the unemployment figures quoted at two millions, it is fatally easy to take this as meaning that two million people are out of work and the rest of the population is comparatively comfortable. I admit that till recently I was in the habit of doing so myself. I used to calculate that if you put the registered unemployed at round about two millions and threw in the destitute and those who for one reason and another were not registered, you might take the number of underfed people in England (for *everyone* on the dole or thereabouts is underfed) as being, at the very most, five millions.
>
> This is an enormous under-estimate, because, in the first place, the only people shown on unemployment figures are those actually drawing the dole – that is, in general, heads of families. An unemployed man's dependants do not figure on the list unless they too are drawing a separate allowance. A Labour Exchange officer told me that to get at the real number of people *living on* (not drawing) the dole, you have got to multiply the official figures by something over three. This alone brings the number of unemployed to round

> about six millions. But in addition there are great numbers of people who are in work but who, from a financial point of view, might equally well be unemployed, because they are not drawing anything that can be described as a living wage. Allow for these and their dependants, throw in as before the old-age pensioners, the destitute, and other nondescripts, and you get an *underfed* population of well over ten millions. [An expert] puts it at twenty millions.
>
> *The Road to Wigan Pier* (Penguin edn, 1962), pp.67–8.

He adds that in Wigan 'more than one person in three . . . is either drawing or living on the dole', and that the army of the jobless includes a 'steady core of from four to five thousand miners who have been continuously unemployed for the past seven years [i.e., since 1929]'.

One result of mass unemployment is visible, as Orwell says, to anyone who uses his eyes as well as in the official reports and statistics: low standards of health and physique stemming from undernourishment. It is true that he sees this not just as a recent phenomenon but as part of a long-term 'physical degeneracy' in England; but conditions had undeniably been worsened by poverty arising from unemployment:

> The physical average in the industrial towns is terribly low, lower even than in London. In Sheffield you have the feeling of walking among a population of troglodytes. The miners are splendid men, but they are usually small, and the mere fact that their muscles are toughened by constant work does not mean that their children start life with a better physique. In any case the miners are physically the pick of the population. The most obvious sign of under-nourishment is the badness of everybody's teeth. In Lancashire you would have to look for a long time before you saw a working-class person with good natural teeth. Indeed, you see very few people with natural teeth at

> all, apart from the children; and even the children's teeth have a frail bluish appearance which means, I suppose, calcium deficiency. Several dentists have told me that in industrial districts a person over thirty with any of his or her own teeth is coming to be an abnormality.
>
> Ibid. pp.86–7.

Poor housing conditions also contributed to low standards of public health:

> As you walk through the industrial towns you lose yourself in labyrinths of little brick houses blackened by smoke, festering in planless chaos round miry alleys and little cindered yards where there are stinking dust-bins and lines of grimy washing and half-ruinous W.C.S. The interiors of these houses are always very much the same, though the number of rooms varies between two or five. All have an almost exactly similar living-room, ten or fifteen feet square, with an open kitchen range; in the larger ones there is a scullery as well, in the smaller ones the sink and copper are in the living-room. At the back there is the yard, or part of a yard shared by a number of houses, just big enough for the dustbin and the W.C. Not a single one has hot water laid on. You might walk, I suppose, through literally hundreds of miles of streets inhabited by miners, every one of whom, when he is in work, gets black from head to foot every day, without ever passing a house in which one could have a bath. It would have been very simple to install a hot-water system working from the kitchen range, but the builder saved perhaps ten pounds on each house by not doing so, and at the time when these houses were built no one imagined that miners wanted baths.
>
> Ibid. p.45.

One of the passages quoted above from J.B. Priestley's book referred to Dickens; and Orwell's description of the 'labyrinths of little brick houses blackened by smoke' will remind some readers of Dickens's *Hard Times* (1854) with its description of conditions in the fictional (but in some respects highly realistic) Lancashire community of Coketown. Victorian parallels also come naturally to mind in relation to the awareness, shared by Priestley, Orwell and others, that England was still, in Disraeli's famous phrase, 'two nations'. To some extent the division was geographical as well as social and economic, as the Victorians themselves recognised. In 1855 Elizabeth Gaskell published a novel entitled *North and South*; and the sense of an invisible line drawn across the middle of England was still strong in the 1930s.

To quote *The Road to Wigan Pier* once more:

> As you travel northward your eye, accustomed to the South or East, does not notice much difference until you are beyond Birmingham. In Coventry you might as well be in Finsbury Park, and the Bull Ring in Birmingham is not unlike Norwich Market, and between all the towns of the Midlands there stretches a villa-civilization indistinguishable from that of the South. It is only when you get a little further north, to the pottery towns and beyond, that you begin to encounter the real ugliness of industrialism – an ugliness so frightful and so arresting that you are obliged, as it were, to come to terms with it.
>
> Op. cit., p.94.

Orwell's account of the ravaged industrial landscape and the hideousness of the urban scene (Sheffield, for instance, has 'a population of half a million and it contains fewer decent buildings than the average East Anglian village of five hundred') is too long to quote here, but well worth looking up (Chapter 7). No wonder that Orwell, who had been educated at Eton and lived in London, concluded that 'when you go to the industrial North you are conscious, quite apart from the unfamiliar scenery, of entering another country'.

The poet W.H. Auden (1907–73) saw physical conditions in the north of England as symbols of class warfare and old antagonisms: it may be possible to believe in the myth of progress if you happen to be comfortably off and living in the south of England,

> But in the north it simply isn't true.
> To those who live in Warrington or Wigan,
> It's not a white lie, it's a whacking big 'un.
>
> There on the old historic battlefield,
> The cold ferocity of human wills,
> The scars of struggle are as yet unhealed;
> Slattern the tenements on sombre hills,
> And gaunt in valleys the square-windowed mills . . .
>
> 'Letter to Lord Byron', *Letters from Iceland*, p.48.

In this same poem Auden, another key-figure for the period, questions the reality of social justice and 'progress' in an age which has 'millions suffering from malnutrition'; and, like Orwell, he moves outwards from contemporary conditions to a historical view of national degeneracy and suggests that the Englishman of the day is

> . . . another man in many ways:
> Ask the cartoonist first, for he knows best.
> Where is the John Bull of the good old days,
> The swaggering bully with the clumsy jest?
> His meaty neck has long been laid to rest,
> His acres of self-confidence for sale;
> He passed away at Ypres and Passchendaele.
>
> Turn to the work of Disney or of Strube;
> There stands our hero in his threadbare seams;
> The bowler hat who straphangs in the tube,
> And kicks the tyrant only in his dreams,
> Trading on pathos, dreading all extremes;

The little Mickey* with the hidden grudge;
Which is the better, I leave you to judge.

Ibid. p.53.

Auden sees popular art as conveying an important truth: the kind of Englishman depicted by Victorian and Edwardian cartoonists perished in the Great War (Ypres and Passchendaele were battles in which huge numbers of young soldiers were slaughtered). Another poet of the same generation, Stephen Spender (b.1909), evokes the inhabitants of 'An Elementary School Classroom in a Slum' as living representatives of the same conditions:

Far far from gusty waves, these children's faces.
Like rootless weeds the torn hair round their paleness.
The tall girl with her weighed-down head. The paper-
Seeming boy with rat's eyes. The stunted unlucky heir
Of twisted bones, reciting a father's gnarled disease,
His lesson from his desk. . . .

Collected Poems 1928–1953 (1955), p.80.

The children described by the middle-class poet towards the end of the decade are the products of unemployment, undernourishment, poor housing and inadequate medical care.

How did this state of affairs come about? The economic crisis, slump, or 'Great Depression', was an international malaise and one that was not quickly cured. After the end of the First World War New York replaced London as the world financial centre; and in the USA a boom began in 1922 that led to frantic speculation and overnight fortunes. This was the 'Jazz Age', of which a characteristic literary document is F. Scott Fitzgerald's *The Great Gatsby* (1925), with a shady

*Mickey Mouse, who has been described as a 'universal icon', is the most famous creation of Walt Disney (1901–66), American maker of animated cartoons, and was introduced to the world in 1928. With Donald Duck (1931), Goofy (1932) and Pluto (1933), Disney's other best-known characters, Mickey Mouse was enormously popular through the Thirties, and few cinema programmes did not include one of these short films. Strube was a newspaper cartoonist.

financier as its central figure. The fever of speculation reached its height in the later twenties; but doubts about the soundness of some of the investments led to a panic on the New York Stock Market, and on a single day (24 October 1929) thirteen million shares changed hands. Many banks and business enterprises failed and many individuals were ruined. The 'Wall Street Crash' inevitably had an effect on British and European economic life, and the cessation of overseas loans by the USA produced a world-wide financial crisis. The shortage of capital led to a fall in exports and in home consumption, and mass unemployment followed. Since the demand for transport had fallen dramatically, areas such as Tyneside which depended heavily on the shipbuilding industry were particularly hard hit.

By August 1932 23 per cent of insured workers in Britain were jobless; the total of unemployed was probably around 3½ million, and the figure continued to be high for several years in spite of some improvement in the economy by the middle of the decade. By 1937 production was actually one-third higher than it had been in 1929, but the number of those unemployed did not fall below one million during the 1930s. There was thus good reason for Orwell to write, in his novel *A Clergyman's Daughter* in the middle of the decade, of 'the great modern commandment – the eleventh commandment which has wiped out all the others: "Thou shalt not lose thy job" ' (Penguin edn, 1960, p.259).

What the creative writers depict in prose and verse is confirmed by the historians and the official records. Two statistical tables bring home forcefully both the appalling conditions in the north of England and the contrast between north and south (see Tables 1 and 2, p. 28).

The Tyneside town of Jarrow, already referred to, became a by-word for mass unemployment, hardship and despair: almost wholly dependent on a single employer, Palmers' shipyards, it

> was reduced to destitution when the yards were closed as part of the restrictionist programme of the shipbuilders. In September 1935, 72.9 per cent of its insured workers were unemployed. A company

Table 1 *Unemployed as Percentage of Insured Workers in Various Regions*

	1929	*1932*	*1937*
London and S.E. England	5.6	13.7	6.4
S.W. England	8.1	17.1	7.8
Midlands	9.3	20.1	7.2
North, N.E., N.W. England	13.5	27.1	13.8
Wales	19.3	36.5	22.3
Scotland	12.1	27.7	15.9
Great Britain	10.5	22.2	10.8
Northern Ireland	15.1	27.2	23.6

Table 2 *Percentage of Insured Workers Unemployed in Distressed and Prosperous Towns, 1934*

Jarrow	67.8	Greater London	8.6
Gateshead	44.2	Birmingham	6.4
Workington	36.3	Coventry	5.1
Maryport	57.0	Oxford	5.1
Abertillery	49.6	Luton	7.7
Merthyr	61.9	High Wycombe	3.3
Greenock	36.3	St. Albans	3.9
Motherwell	37.4	Watford	7.0

From C. L. Mowat, *Britain between the Wars 1918–1940* (Methuen edn, 1968) pp.464–5.

> proposed to construct on the site of the shipyards an integrated steelworks. . . . The scheme came to nothing. . . . Thereupon, the townspeople and the town council organised a march of 200 Jarrow men to London in October 1936, with the aid of Ellen Wilkinson, the local M.P.; they carried petitions asking the government to provide work for the area.
>
> Mowat, p.443.

The march of the unemployed from Jarrow to London seized the popular imagination, but was only the climax of a long period of severe distress, and Ellen Wilkinson's later account under the title *The Town that was Murdered* (1939) describes the 'utterly stagnant' condition of the community in 1932–3 – that is, three or four years before the march:

> In Middlesbrough I had thought that I had known what poverty could mean. But in that town some industry was going on, some people had work. Compared to Jarrow, things on Tees-side were moving. Jarrow in that year, 1932–3, was utterly stagnant. There was no work. No one had a job, except a few railwaymen, officials, the workers in the co-operative Stores, and the few clerks and craftsmen who went out of the town to their jobs each day. The unemployment rate was over 80 per cent.
>
> *The Town that was Murdered* (1939), pp.191–2.

The origins and purpose of the march are described in Ellen Wilkinson's book:

> All the respectable deputations had got nowhere. At a great demonstration of the unemployed [in Jarrow], Councillor David Riley, as chairman, suggested that the unemployed of Jarrow should march to London, and tell the people of England on their way down of the treatment they had received. . . . Hunger marches of desperate men from the distressed areas there had been in plenty. The comfortable had dismissed these efforts as 'communist demonstrations', as though that accounted for everything. But the fact that the Town Council sanctioned the march, practically unanimously, meant that appeals for support were sent out over the signature of the Mayor. When the time table had been worked out, the letters asking for the use of halls and services were sent to the towns on the way, not by a March Committee but on official Borough notepaper over the signature of the Town Clerk. . . .
>
> It was decided that the marchers should arrive in London for the opening of the new session of Parliament; that a petition signed by as many citizens of Jarrow as possible should be prepared; and that it

> should be carried by the marchers on the way, being handed to the Chief Magistrate of each town in which the marchers halted for the night for his safe keeping. Not Parliament alone was the object of the march . . . but the rousing of public opinion in England to the plight of Jarrow and the forgotten areas like it.
>
> Ibid. pp.198–9.

Something of the spirit in which the march was undertaken is conveyed by her account, still graphic after fifty years, of its beginning:

> Prayers were said for the marchers that Sunday of October 4, 1936, in every church and chapel in Jarrow. On Monday morning the men lined up for a final review by the Mayor outside the Town Hall. The men had done their best to look smart on the little they had. Faces carefully shaved . . . but so thin. Broken boots mended and polished. Shabby clothes brushed and mended by their wives. The waterproof cape rolled over the shoulder bandolier fashion. We marched to Christ Church for a short service, which the men's wives and the Mayor and Corporation attended. The words of that grave and saintly man, Bishop Gordon of Jarrow, as he pronounced the blessing and bade us Godspeed gave to the men and their wives a sense of high purpose in their Crusade.
>
> Ibid. pp.200–1.

As these extracts suggest, 'hunger marches' at least had the effect of bringing home to the relatively affluent the plight of many of their countrymen: A.J.P. Taylor points out that, whereas the demonstrations in London were 'to little purpose', the progress of the marchers through the country was

> a propaganda stroke of great effect. The hunger marchers displayed the failure of capitalism in a way that mere figures or literary description could not. Middle-class people felt the call of conscience. They set up

> soup-kitchens for the marchers and accommodated them in local schools.
>
> Op. cit., p.433.

Efforts by the government were small-scale and largely unavailing:

> In November 1934 they acknowledged the existence of four Depressed or, as the Lords tactfully renamed them, Special Areas – Scotland, South Wales, West Cumberland and Tyneside. Two commissioners were appointed to revive these areas, with an initial grant of £2 million. Not much came of this. The old industries could not be pulled back to life by a little judicious prodding. In 1936 the English commissioner, Sir Malcolm Stewart, reported that he had 'generally speaking . . . failed'. He wanted powers with which to attract new industries. His successor was given these powers in 1937; and industrial estates were started in South Wales and near Gateshead. In all, work was found for 12,000 men, an unimpressive total.
>
> Taylor, p.436.

Jarrow is the best remembered of the communities devastated by unemployment, but it was of course far from being an isolated case. Another historian cites the case of the Bishop Auckland area of south-west Durham:

> It had had 33 coal pits employing 28,000 miners. By 1935 17 pits were abandoned, three more closed and unlikely to reopen, and the remaining 13, where work dragged on with small and irregular shifts, employed 6500 men, though often not on full time. Despite the fact that many families, and particularly the younger men, had moved away, unemployment was very high: 80 per cent or more of the workers in Tow Law were unemployed, almost 100 per cent of those in Shildon; at West Auckland only one hundred men out of a thousand had had work in the last seven years. In a

> street of sixty cottages in one of the mining villages you would hardly find one where the man was at work.
>
> Mowat, pp.481–2.

The same writer estimates that during this period between 15 per cent and 30 per cent of the population of Great Britain were below or near the poverty-line (one enquirer found that the property, furniture and savings of eight million families were worth less than £100); 10 per cent of the population (20 per cent of the children) were very badly fed, and 50 per cent not properly nourished; infant mortality and the death rate from tuberculosis were higher in areas of mass unemployment than in the relatively prosperous south-east. Large numbers received 'dole' payments subject to the notorious 'means test':

> No doubt any means test would have been resented by men who believed, not without justice, that their lack of work was not their own fault; what made the means test hated and loathed by the working classes was its form and its administration. It was a household means test. It took account of any earnings by members of the household (sons and daughters, for instance) as well as of savings, pensions, income from house property or other assets. Thrift was penalised and improvidence rewarded. Family solidarity was undermined: growing sons and daughters were forced to support their parents in a way which frayed the tempers of both generations and might break up the family: sons and daughters would move into lodgings in order not to be 'dragged down' by having to support their parents. The test was an encouragement to the tattle-tale and the informer, the writer of anonymous letters and the local blackmailer; to all sorts of unneighbourliness. It stimulated petty tyranny and insolence on the part of Labour Exchange clerks and managers; the weekly visit to the Exchange would bring the sudden, curt announcement by the clerk: 'They've knocked you off dole.'
>
> Mowat, pp.483–4.

Walter Greenwood's novel *Love on the Dole* (1933; also successful in adaptations for the stage and cinema) contains a classic account of working-class life during the period. Greenwood's hero, Harry Hardcastle, grows up in Hanky Park, a working-class neighbourhood in a depressed northern city. (The author himself had grown up in Salford.) On leaving school he serves an apprenticeship in an engineering firm – a system that, in practice, provides a supply of cheap labour; but as soon as his period of apprenticeship comes to an end, he finds himself out of work. The life and background of Harry and his family, and of millions of others in 'Hanky Park' and elsewhere, are described in the novel by a radical orator:

> '. . .And to find the cost of this present system you have only to look at our own lives and the lives of our parents and their parents. Labour never ending, constant struggles to pay the rent and to buy sufficient food and clothing; no time for anything that is bright and beautiful. We never see such things. All we see are these grey depressing streets; mile after mile of them; never ending. . . And the houses in which we are compelled to live are as though they have been designed by fiends in hell for our especial punishment. When work is regular we are just able to live from week to week: there is no surplus. But for ever, there hangs over us that dread threat of unemployment. Unemployment that can and does reduce most honest working folk to pauperdom, that saddles them with a debt that takes years to repay. Even at its best I say that this is not life. And it is not the lot of one or two individual families. Look around you here in Hanky Park; not a part but the whole of it is so affected. This existence is what is fobbed off on to us as Life. . . .'
>
> *Love on the Dole* (Penguin edn, 1986) p.86.

In the following passage Greenwood describes the scene in

which the unemployed sign on for their dole payments:

> [Harry] stood in a long queue of shabby men, hands in pockets, staring fixedly and unseeing at the ground. At street corners, leaning against house walls or squatting on the kerb-stones, were more men, clothes stinking of age, waiting until the queue opposite went into the building when they would take their places in forming another. And all through the day, every quarter-hour, would see another crowd of fresh faces coming to sign the unemployed register at their appointed times.
>
> Ibid. pp.153–4.

In the same scene the physical setting reinforces the picture of human despair, and the writer's crude but effective symbolism implies that the lives of the poor are reduced almost to the level of brute beasts:

> An erstwhile reformatory school for erring boys, an ugly, barrack-like building, serves as one of the Two Cities' labour exchanges. Hemmed in on three sides by slums, tenements and doss houses, the remaining side stares at the gas works and a cattle-loading mound, into, and out of which, bleating sheep, cows and bulls, their eyes rolling, their parched tongues lolling, are driven by loutish men and cowed dogs. And the slum children, seeing in the inoffensive creatures a means to exercise their own animal instincts, come out of their dens armed with whips and sticks and stones to belabour the animals as they pass, meanwhile indulging in the most hideous inhuman screams, shouts and howls such as occasions horror in the mind of a sympathetic observer and, doubtless, terrified bewilderment on the parts of the doomed beasts as they, smarting under whip, stick and stone, run blindly along the dinning unfamiliar streets finally to find themselves packed, suffocatingly, in wretched cattle trucks.

> A high wall, enclosing an asphalt yard, ran round the building. On it was scrawled in chalk, and in letters a foot high: 'Unemployed Mass Meeting Today 3 o'clock.' The handiwork of Communists five or six weeks ago.
>
> Ibid. p.153.

When the infamous Means Test (the subject of a book by Walter Brierley, *Means Test Man*, 1935) is introduced, the dole ceases for those who can (in theory at least) be supported by their relatives. One of Harry's friends is turned out of his home for this reason, and after a spell in a doss-house (a place recalling Orwell's stark reporting of similar scenes) joins the army in desperation:

> 'Ain't y' heard? He's joined th' army cause he had to.'
>
> 'Had to?' repeated Harry.
>
> 'Aye, bloody well had to. His pa kicked him out o' th' 'ouse when he was knocked off dole. Told him t' clear out 'n join th' army cause he wasn't gonna keep him. He wus livin' i' one o' them doss houses i' Garden Place. Poor devil couldn't afford price of a bed. Tuk him all his time t' find for a tupp'ny leanover.'
>
> Harry gazed at Jack, puzzled: 'Tupp'ny leanover. Wha' d'y' mean?'
>
> Jack shrugged: 'Y' should go 'n have a luk at it. It's for t' real down and outs as can't afford price of a bed. They charge y' tuppence t' lean o'er a rope all night. Hell, y' should see 'em. About forty blokes sittin' on forms in a line an' leanin' o'er a rope . . . elbow t' elbow swayin' fast asleep, except the old bastards who're dyin' and can't sleep for spittin' an' coughin' their guts away. . . .
>
> Ibid. p.231.

When Harry's sister falls in love, even instinctive feelings are blighted by the squalid conditions in which their life is passed: as she and her lover stand in the street talking,

They regarded each other, fascinated, amazed, inarticulate. She whispered his name ardently, kissed him again and would have again, but for a couple of men, who, pausing at the street corner, stood conversing. She glared at them.

'Let's go round the back, Larry,' she murmured.

His spirits contracted on the instant; the magic trickled away.

A back entry for a love bower! A three-foot wide passage, house backs and backyard walls crowding either side; stagnating puddles in the broken flagging; the sounds of the traffic of people's visiting the stinking privies, and, hark, over the roof-tops, the sound of a cracked voice singing shrilly. Mrs Dorbell's, the old hag, who, when drunk, always chose the privy seat on which to sing the same song:

'We'll laugh and sing an' we'll drive away care;
Ah've enough for meself an' a likkle bit t'spare.
If a nice yeng man should ride my way
Oooow, Ah'll make him as welcome as the flowers
in May!'

He could imagine the expression of glass-eyed vacuity on Mrs Dorbell's face. His arm, round Sal's waist, relaxed. He could feel the dulling sense of utter hopelessness creeping over him.

Ibid. pp.148–9.

Despite some crudities of construction and style and some melodramatic and sentimental clichés, Greenwood's novel has not lost its power after half a century and speaks from its period for a huge mass of people who were almost entirely without a public voice to express the daily circumstances of their bitterly hard lives.

While some writers of the period give a bleakly pessimistic picture of conditions, a few are stirred by the conviction that change is possible by mass action. The Communist author Lewis Jones, in his novel *Cwmardy* (1937), depicts a successful strike by Welsh miners. Like the Jarrow march, the strike is begun almost in the spirit of a religious crusade:

> Down on the rubbish dump thousands of miners and their womenfolk were waiting for the meeting to begin. . . . A lorry in the centre of the huge mass of people held Ezra and some other men. Presently a glorious baritone lifted itself from the throng in the lilting melody of an old Welsh hymn. Its strains floated over the crowd like a shawl encircling a child. The people lost their individual identities in the vibrating rhythm of the tune which impelled their emotions into expression through bonds of vocal unity. In a matter of seconds every voice had taken up the refrain. . . .
>
> The men on the platform stood with bared heads and took part in the singing until it finished, when they all, with the exception of Ezra, sat down. . . . Each of the thousands of eyes was fixed upon him when his cold voice split the air as he reported all that had happened since the previous meeting. With steady calculation he built his case against the company and eventually concluded with the words:
>
> 'That is the position, fellow workmen, either we fight or starve. You will yourselves decide which.'
>
> For a minute after his voice ceased the whole world seemed to slumber, then it awoke to a terrific shout that rattled and throbbed in the blood of the people present. It ascended in increasing crescendos, pushing itself up the mountain with brazen resonance until it banged itself against the windows of the Big House.
>
> 'Strike! Strike!'
>
> *Cwmardy* (1937), pp.84–5.

As Carole Snee has said, 'It is the strike which galvanises the collective will of the community and reveals to individuals, not their own power, but the power of the class to which they belong' ('Working-class Literature or Proletarian Writing?', *Culture and Crisis in Britain in the 30s*, ed. J. Clark, M. Heinemann, D. Margolies and C. Snee, 1979, p.185).

Jones's reference to the miners' 'womenfolk' recalls Orwell's point that, while the statistics refer mainly to unemployed men, the burden of hardship was suffered at least equally by their wives and families. It was natural that most of the unemployed should be men in a period when women normally relinquished paid employment after marriage; and many accounts stress the plight of unemployed males during these years of dole queues and indefinite lounging on street corners. As a corrective to this somewhat one-sided picture may be cited a remarkable account of the conditions of life for women, given by the social reformer Margery Spring-Rice in her book *Working-Class Wives* (1939). Between 1923 and 1933, the maternal mortality rate (i.e., deaths in pregnancy and childbirth, and from related causes) actually rose by 22 per cent. This and other factors led to the formation in 1933 of the Women's Health Enquiry Committee, a non-political group which set out to investigate the health of women, especially married working-class women. Questionnaires were administered, and analysis of the replies returned by 1250 women showed that 'the conditions of life [of the women concerned] . . . are such as to make it impossible to maintain after marriage the standard (often low enough) of health and well-being which was possible to them as unmarried working girls and would be possible to them still if their incomes were fantastically larger' (*Working-Class Wives*, Virago edn, 1981, p.26). The statistics provided show clearly that health was closely related to income, and that poor health was very common among working-class women after the birth of their first child.

The conditions in which these women of the Thirties lived and brought up their families are highlighted by the contrast in the situation a generation or two later: for example, 'out of every thousand babies born alive in England and Wales in 1939, 50.6 were dead before they were a year old, whereas in 1977 the corresponding figure had dropped to below 14; and comparable reductions have also been achieved throughout the years of early childhood' (Barbara Wootton, Introduction to Second Edition of *Working-Class Wives* (1981), p.iv). In the Thirties tuberculosis was the principal cause of deaths in early adult life (according to Ellen Wilkinson, 'The average proportion of deaths of children in Jarrow from all forms of tuberculosis was found to be 24.4, the corresponding figure for all children in urban districts of England and Wales being 10.5 per cent'). This tragic picture of ill-health and early death was transformed by the advent of the National Health Service, in operation from 1948 following the Beveridge Report of 1942, by advances in medical science and the discovery of new drugs such as penicillin, and by the extension of social services; but in the Thirties most of these developments were still in the future:

> For children between one and five, measles and pneumonia (plus whooping cough for girls) were the main killers, followed by diphtheria, and for children of school age diphtheria was the chief cause, closely followed by accidents in the case of the boys. In early adult life tuberculosis headed the list, and 15 per cent of deaths throughout the population were due to tuberculosis and other infectious diseases.
>
> Op. cit., p.xii.

Mass unemployment, as we have seen, brought widespread poverty and suffering. Poverty was, of course, nothing new in England, and some accounts suggest that the world of the destitute evoked by Dickens in the mid-nineteenth century had not entirely disappeared in the England of the 1930s. At the extreme of destitution some of the unemployed helped to swell the number of vagrants and homeless; and tramps were a familiar sight in towns and cities and on the road. In an essay, 'Common Lodging Houses', published in the left-wing weekly *New Statesman & Nation* on 3 September 1932, Orwell described from first-hand observation the squalid premises inhabited by the unemployed or those on very low incomes:

> The dormitories are horrible fetid dens, packed with anything up to a hundred men. . . . As often as not the beds are verminous, and the kitchens invariably swarm with cockroaches or black beetles.

Conditions in the lodging-houses run by charitable organisations such as the Salvation Army were better than in those run for profit, but a rigid and uncongenial discipline was enforced; so that, as Orwell says, the choice was between 'an easy-going pigsty and a hygienic prison'.

In the following year in *Down and Out in Paris and London* (1933) Orwell gave a much fuller account of the life of tramps and beggars in London lodging-houses and casual wards. In order to learn how life was actually lived in such circumstances, he dressed as a tramp – and discovered in the process how much difference dress and appearance made to social attitudes and behaviour:

> I stayed in the streets till late at night, keeping on the move all the time. Dressed as I was, I was half afraid that the police might arrest me as a vagabond, and I dared not speak to anyone, imagining that they must notice a disparity between my accent and my clothes. (Later I discovered that this never happened.) My new clothes had put me instantly into a new world. Everyone's demeanour seemed to have changed abruptly. I helped a hawker pick up a barrow that he had upset. 'Thanks, mate,' he said with a grin. No one had called me mate before in my life – it was the clothes that had done it. For the first time I noticed, too, how the attitude of women varies with a man's clothes. When a badly dressed man passes them they shudder away from him with a quite frank movement of disgust, as though he were a dead cat. Clothes are powerful things. Dressed in a tramp's clothes it is very difficult, at any rate for the first day, not to feel that you are genuinely degraded. You might feel the same shame, irrational but very real, your first night in prison.
>
> *Down and Out in Paris and London* (Secker & Warburg edn, 1954), p.129.

At the cost of one shilling, he spends the night in a 'doss-house':

> I paid the shilling, and the boy led me up a rickety unlighted staircase to a bedroom. It had a sweetish

reek of paregoric and foul linen; the windows seemed to be tight shut, and the air was almost suffocating at first. There was a candle burning, and I saw that the room measured fifteen feet square by eight high, and had eight beds in it. Already six lodgers were in bed, queer lumpy shapes with all their own clothes, even their boots, piled on top of them. Someone was coughing in a loathsome manner in one corner.

When I got into the bed I found that it was as hard as a board, and as for the pillow, it was a mere hard cylinder like a block of wood. It was rather worse than sleeping on a table, because the bed was not six feet long, and very narrow, and the mattress was convex, so that one had to hold on to avoid falling out. The sheets stank so horribly of sweat that I could not bear them near my nose. Also, the bedclothes only consisted of the sheets and a cotton counterpane, so that though stuffy it was none too warm. Several noises recurred throughout the night. About once in an hour the man on my left – a sailor, I think – woke up, swore vilely, and lighted a cigarette. Another man, victim of a bladder disease, got up and noisily used his chamber-pot half a dozen times during the night. The man in the corner had a coughing fit once in every twenty minutes, so regularly that one came to listen for it as one listens for the next yap when a dog is baying the moon. It was an unspeakably repellent sound; a foul bubbling and retching, as though the man's bowels were being churned up within him. Once when he struck a match I saw that he was a very old man, with a grey, sunken face like that of a corpse, and he was wearing his trousers wrapped round his head as a nightcap, a thing which for some reason disgusted me very much. Every time he coughed or the other man swore, a sleepy voice from one of the other beds cried out:

'Shut up! Oh, for Christ's – *sake* shut up!'

Ibid. pp.130–1.

Again we seem to be back in Dickens's London. Orwell

estimated the number of tramps in England at 'tens of thousands', and quotes figures published by the London County Council on the basis of a census conducted on the night of 13 February 1931: 60 men and 18 women were 'spending the night in the streets'; 1057 men and 137 women were 'in shelters and homes not licensed as common lodging-houses'; 88 men and 12 women were 'in the crypt of St Martin's-in-the-Fields Church [in Trafalgar Square]' (p.203). As Orwell points out, the figures for those sleeping in the open air are likely to be an underestimate.

It is true that the picture in this decade was not one of unrelieved gloom, and any fair account of the Thirties must include some reference to more hopeful developments. For example, as already noted in the Introduction, the governments of the Thirties initiated an extensive programme of slum clearance and rehousing (as C.L. Mowat says, 'Until 1930 slum clearance was hardly tackled at all'). There were also some significant improvements in diet and health. By the middle of the decade, the national economic situation had already improved markedly. To quote A.J.P. Taylor again:

> In 1934 [Neville] Chamberlain [Chancellor of the Exchequer in Ramsay Macdonald's government] announced that the country had finished the story of Bleak House and could now sit down to enjoy the first chapter of Great Expectations. . . . Chamberlain reduced the standard rate of income tax to 4s 6d., restored the cut in unemployment benefit and half the cut in government and local government salaries. In 1935 he claimed: 'Broadly speaking we may say that we have recovered in this country 80 per cent of our prosperity'. The claim was unduly modest. Production was ten points higher than in 1929; wage rates had fallen since then by 3 per cent, the cost of living by 13 per cent.
>
> Op. cit., p.435.

Yet, as Taylor also notes, 'Mass unemployment in the old industrial areas still clouded this cheerful picture': as we have already seen, the Jarrow march took place two years after Chamberlain's promise of 'great expectations'. The truth was that there were still marked regional and class disparities in recovery and prosperity, as there always had been. At the beginning of the decade the number of working-class people in Liverpool subsisting below the poverty line was nearly twice the figure for London. The expert in nutrition, Sir John Boyd Orr, noted that the average height of fourteen-year-old boys at a public school was nearly six inches greater than for boys at a council school: a striking index of the different conditions in which different classes lived.

These conditions are, as we have seen, reflected in the work of some of the writers of the period; and the literary response includes a variety of reactions ranging from despair to protest, from escapism to a passionate demand for reform. The response, it is worth noting, is largely from observers and commentators who were themselves of the middle classes: though there is a good deal of writing *about* the working class, there is, in this or any other period, relatively little working-class literature in the sense that it was written *by* members of that class. As Bernard Bergonzi has noted, the most influential group of young English writers in the Thirties

> shared important formative experiences: being sons of the English or Anglo-Irish professional or administrative class, very conscious of the First World War but too young to fight in it; educated at boarding schools and, in nearly all cases, at Oxford or Cambridge.
>
> *Reading the Thirties* (1978), p.2.

The writers Bergonzi has in mind are the poets W.H. Auden, Stephen Spender, Cecil Day Lewis, John Betjeman, John Lehmann and Louis MacNeice, and the novelists Christopher Isherwood, Edward Upward, Evelyn Waugh, Graham Greene, George Orwell, Anthony Powell, Cyril Connolly and Henry Green; some of these have already been referred to, and there will be occasion to cite most of the others in the course of this study. As Bergonzi says, their class and educational background was 'strikingly homogeneous': only

Orwell had not been to Oxford or Cambridge, and he was an Old Etonian.

One of the best of Orwell's essays is titled 'How the Poor Die'; and he is the best literary witness of the period to how the poor live. A few years after his graphic and sickening description of London lodging-houses and casual wards in *Down and Out in Paris and London*, Orwell published his novel, *Keep the Aspidistra Flying* (1936), in the opening chapter of which two tramps enter a bookshop and then shamble out again:

> Gordon watched them go. They were just by-products. The throw-outs of the money-god. All over London, by tens of thousands, draggled old beasts of that description; creeping like unclean beetles to the grave.
>
> *Keep the Aspidistra Flying* (Penguin edn, 1962), p.21.

For Orwell's anti-hero, Gordon Comstock, these sordid and pathetic figures induce a more generalised depression:

> He gazed out at the graceless street. At this moment it seemed to him that in a street like this, in a town like this, every life that is lived must be meaningless and intolerable. The sense of disintegration, of decay, that is endemic in our time, was strong upon him.
>
> Ibid.

Comstock's disgust is provoked not only by the mechanical, indifferent mode of life enforced by the city (there is a reference later to 'the strap-hanging army that sways eastward at morning, westward at night, in the carriages of the Underground') but by the underlying political and economic system. He sees all aspects of life, even the most personal, as depending on the cash nexus – not only work and social life, but even courtship and marriage:

> 'But I say, Gordon, look here. This girl, Miss – Miss Waterlow, did you say her name was? – Rose-

mary; doesn't she care for you at all, really?'

Gordon's conscience pricked him, though not very deeply. He could not say that Rosemary did not care for him.

'Oh, yes, she does care for me. In her own way, I dare say she cares for me quite a lot. But not enough, don't you see. She can't, while I've got no money. It's all money.'

'But surely money isn't so important as all that? After all, there *are* other things.'

'What other things? Don't you see that a man's whole personality is bound up with his income? His personality *is* his income. How can you be attractive to a girl when you've got no money? You can't wear decent clothes, you can't take her out to dinner or to the theatre or away for week-ends, you can't carry a cheery, interesting atmosphere about with you. And it's rot to say that kind of thing doesn't matter. It does. If you haven't got money there isn't even anywhere where you can meet. Rosemary and I never meet except in the streets or in picture galleries. She lives in some foul women's hostel, and my bitch of a landlady won't allow women in the house. Wandering up and down beastly wet streets – that's what Rosemary associates me with. Don't you see how it takes the gilt off everything?'

Ibid., p.102.

Comstock's reaction to urban life and to the conscripted 'army' of commuters is a recurring motif in the period that takes many forms. Louis MacNeice (1907–63), for instance, in his poem 'Birmingham', written in October 1933, contemplates the crowds of factory-workers:

. . . the factory chimneys on sullen sentry will all night
  wait
To call, in the harsh morning, sleep-stupid faces
  through the daily gate.

and the employees whose minds are numbed by boredom:

> The lunch hour: the shops empty, shopgirls' faces relax
> Diaphanous as green glass empty as old almanacs . . .

The same poem draws attention to the visual and social contrasts to be found in a large city:

> . . . the streets run away between the proud glass of shops
> Cubical scent-bottles artificial legs arctic foxes and electric mops
> But beyond this centre the slumward vista thins like a diagram:
> There, unvisited, are Vulcan's forges who doesn't care a tinker's damn.
>
> *Collected Poems* (Faber edn, 1979), pp.17–18.

In the city centre are the displays of mainly luxury goods in the shop-windows, but in the grimy suburbs are the heavy industrial neighbourhoods where things are actually made.

Another poet, John Betjeman (1906–84), expresses a more violent distaste for the prosperous and 'progressive' town of Slough:

> Come, friendly bombs, and fall on Slough
> It isn't fit for humans now,
> There isn't grass to graze a cow
> Swarm over, Death!
>
> Come, bombs, and blow to smithereens
> Those air-conditioned, bright canteens,
> Tinned fruit, tinned meat, tinned milk, tinned beans
> Tinned minds, tinned breath. . . .
>
> *John Betjeman's Collected Poems* (1958), p.21.

Betjeman's anger is mainly aesthetic in origin: it is the sterile impersonality of a flourishing modern town, and the absence of tradition and atmosphere, that he deplores, and his protest has a familiar ring, being essentially that of a Victorian critic of society such as Ruskin. What this exasperated little poem fails to take into account is that the prosperity of a town in the South of England such as Slough was, in the Thirties, a matter for thankfulness rather than disapproval. The unemployed of Jarrow, or any other northern town, would have been glad to share Slough's brightness, optimism and affluence.

In one of the best of his early novels, *A Gun for Sale* (1936), Graham Greene (b.1904) evokes the drabness of a Midland city ('Nottwich' is based on Nottingham, where Greene had worked as a journalist) as a train pulls into the station after a comfortless overnight journey:

> There was no dawn that day in Nottwich. Fog lay over the city like a night sky with no stars. The air in the streets was clear. You have only to imagine that it was night. The first tram crawled out of its shed and took the steel track down towards the market. An old piece of newspaper blew up against the door of the Royal Theatre and flattened out. In the streets on the outskirts of Nottwich nearest the pits an old man plodded by with a pole tapping at the windows. The stationer's window in the High Street was full of Prayer Books and Bibles: a printed card remained among them, a relic of Armistice Day, like the old drab wreath of Haig poppies by the War Memorial: 'Look up, and swear by the slain of the war that you'll never forget.' Along the line a signal lamp winked green in the dark day and the lit carriages drew slowly in past the cemetery, the glue factory, over the wide tidy cement-lined river. A bell began to ring from the Roman Catholic cathedral. A whistle blew.
>
> The packed train moved slowly into another morning: smuts were thick on all the faces, everyone had slept in his clothes.
>
> *A Gun for Sale* (Penguin edn, 1972, pp.40–1).

Again it should be noted that, historically viewed, such protests belong to a long line of anti-urban writing that goes back to the early stages of the Industrial Revolution and extends from the Romantic poets (as in Wordsworth's sonnet 'The world is too much with us'), through the Victorian social critics such as Carlyle, Ruskin and Morris and the urban novelists from Dickens to Gissing, to T. S. Eliot's *The Waste Land* (1922) and Patrick Hamilton's eloquently titled trilogy of novels *Twenty Thousand Streets Under the Sky* (1935). But social conditions in the Thirties gave a new sharpness and urgency to familiar diagnoses of the ills of urban and industrial society.

With these last quotations we have moved away from the central and specific problems of unemployment and poverty to a more generalised sense of malaise, a conviction that something is grievously amiss in society as a whole. The optimism that normally follows the conclusion of a period of war – not only the belief that, in the phrase of the time, a 'war to end wars' had been won, but the hope that a new society could be created that was, in another popular phrase, 'fit for heroes to live in' – had been felt in 1918. But by the Thirties it had given way to a sense of angry resentment or bitter despair. Contrasting reactions to the period are to be found in, on the one hand, the early novels of Evelyn Waugh and Anthony Powell, with their picture of the hedonistic younger generation of the upper classes, and, on the other hand, in the writings of politically committed writers of the period, especially those who espoused Marxism and Communism, with their idealistic quest for far-reaching change, if necessary through revolution. These reactions, which suggest the wide range of response to the contemporary situation that was possible on the part of writers and intellectuals, are considered in the next chapter.

2 'Ferocious theologies'

According to W. W. Robson, the Thirties were preoccupied with ideologies: 'Where the twenties had been indifferent to political or religious commitments, the thirties were obsessed with them' (*Modern English Literature* (1970), p.125). Such generalisations, lumping together all social groups and age groups, obviously admit of numerous exceptions, but there is plenty of evidence that the quest on the part of thinking people for a faith adequate to the age in which they lived took on a new urgency at that time. Such a quest, which had been a feature of intellectual and spiritual life since the Victorian period, became more imperious in response to the problems and menaces of these years. In this chapter we shall consider some of the evidence that suggests a variety of responses to this felt need.

Politically, there was a notable growth in left-wing sympathies, ranging from the moderate to the extreme. Publications such as the *Left Review*, founded in 1934, which had a Marxist bias, and John Lehmann's *New Writing*, founded in 1936, which idealistically encouraged working-class authors and readers, reached relatively small audiences; but a more significant sign of the times was the influential Left Book Club formed in May 1936 by the well-established publisher Victor Gollancz. Its programme was to resist the rise of Nazism and Fascism by providing 'the indispensable basis of *knowledge* without which a really effective United Front of all men and women cannot be built'. It made topical and controversial books available to members at a small price (its most enduring title was Orwell's *The Road to Wigan Pier*), and its membership was about 50 000. Furthermore,

> the books were not only sold – they were read and discussed in the Left Book Club groups which sprang up almost spontaneously, five hundred within a year, and of which there were at the peak some twelve hundred in existence. Most of these groups had a wide

> mixture of members, socially and politically, and they tended to be strongest and most active in areas where the official political parties of the left were weak – notably in the outer suburbs of London and other cities, hitherto considered politically Conservative, as well as in smaller country towns and villages. Often they branched out into organising meetings, Spanish or Russian film shows, Aid for Spain and so on. The Left Book Club had the kind of energy and local initiative that later marked the early years of the Campaign for Nuclear Disarmament.
>
> (Noreen Branson and Margot Heinemann, *Britain in the Nineteen Thirties*, 1971, p.277).

Although the Left Book Club continued into the forties, its period of greatest influence was 1936–8, and (as the same authors say) 'for a whole generation it had meant a unique and irreversible process of socialist education' (p.278). At the same time it was for the Labour Party something of an embarrassment and an irritation, since the Club's stance was noticeably further to the left than their own. To quote A.J.P. Taylor,

> It had always been a critical problem for Labour how to win strong middle-class support, and the party had counted on foreign affairs to do this. Now the Left Book Club was diverting highminded school teachers into reading Communist tracts when they ought to have been joining the Labour party and working for it.
>
> Op. cit., p.488.

But it was not only middle-class professional people who were attracted by Communist ideals and Communist propaganda, for the sympathies of many younger writers and intellectuals at this time moved in the same direction. A spokesman for revolutionary idealism was Michael Roberts (1902–48), editor of two anthologies, *New Signatures* (1932) and *New Country* (1933), with contributions by Auden, Day Lewis, Isherwood, Spender and others. In his introduction to the latter volume Roberts writes:

> I think, and the writers in this book obviously agree, that there is only one way of life for us: to renounce that system [i.e., capitalism] now and to live by fighting against it.

He insists that 'It is time that those who would conserve something which is still valuable in England began to see that only a revolution can save their standards' and accuses his opponents of living in a fool's paradise:

> But if you, reader, stand for the accepted order; if you cannot envisage a state in which resources are used to meet the needs of the community and not for individual profit, please remember that the Union Jack, the British Grenadiers, and cricket are not your private property. They are ours. Your proper emblem is a balance sheet. You're a fool if you think your system will give you cricket much longer. . . .

The Communist Party of Great Britain had been founded as early as 1920, and Auden, Isherwood and others came into contact with Communist doctrines and organisations during their periods of residence in Germany. The Soviet Union was looked to as a model and strenuously advertised as such by some writers and propagandists of the period: a book by Sidney and Beatrice Webb, for instance, hailed it as 'a new civilisation'. Looking back on his own earlier beliefs, John Lehmann in his autobiography explains both the appeal of the Russian example and the failure to perceive its defects:

> The factors we missed were missed by thousands who did not hold our views. It did not occur to us that the dynamic released by Hitler's revolution might be more anti-rational than anti-Russian, or that Wotan and Marx were capable, at a given moment, of finding the democrats and imperialists of the West more contemptible than one another. We never imagined, having seen the reforming régimes collapse, that a solution to the endemic crisis of monopoly capitalism other than Marx's revolution might be found. We missed the absurdity of the apocalyptic nature of the

Communist doctrine – an absurdity that had long become clear to such canny and cynical dictators as Stalin. None of us, not even George Orwell, had as yet grasped the fact that in the proletarian paradise all citizens might be equal in theory – but some 'were more equal than others'. And we astonishingly deluded ourselves into believing that Moscow had not only established all those liberties and opportunities that were the breath of our being, but had established them beyond the possibility of destruction.

The delusion that 'Moscow, of all places, was the sole source of light' came partly from wish-dreaming; partly from the absence of adequate facts on which to base our views (the facts were to come thick and fast in the next decade for those who had eyes open enough to see them); and partly from the extremely skilful and widely ramified propaganda emanating from Moscow. In Russia itself, one might have thought, one would see the facts for what they were; but once across the border at Negoreloye the propaganda was non-stop and exclusive, and so intense that it was difficult to remain in a frame of mind where one could coolly question; besides, there was much to be applauded and much that was absorbingly interesting, and on these features one's visitor-eyes were carefully directed.

Lehmann recalls what he saw, and what he failed to see, on a visit to Russia in 1934:

What one saw was a Welfare State being built up with heady Slavonic enthusiasm, backward compared with the Welfare State we have since created in Britain but starting from much further back. What one did not see then were the moral and intellectual conditions of the material progress: the total absence of political freedom, the fatal lack of open critical check in bureaucratic one-party government, the concealed poisoning of truth and corruption of values, the paralysing power of the secret police which produced

> one kind of life for those who were not suspect to the régime, and another of the most cruel and unjust order for those who were. In 1934, when I made my first trip to Russia, there was an impetus and zest to Socialist planning in such marked contrast to the economic stagnation and political despair of the Austria from which I had come, that it was impossible not to feel there was 'something in it'. This active optimism excused for me spectacles of poverty in the outskirts of the big cities as squalid as any in Vienna; the development of a privileged class one couldn't fail to notice in the course of long journeys in trains with their sharply distinguished levels of comfort; and the electric-light switches that didn't work, the plugs that didn't pull, and the taps that came away in one's hands in the new hotels into which one was ushered with such a flourish of pride. In the future lay the Trials, the new terror (old terror admitted as soon as a new one started), the betrayal of the Spanish War and the Nazi–Soviet Pact, not to be guessed at that time.
>
> *The Whispering Gallery* (1955), pp.218–19.

Twenty years later, and with a fuller knowledge not only of subsequent history but of what was really happening in Stalin's Russia, the note of disillusion is strong; and a book that brings together the collective testimony of several writers, British, European and American, who underwent a similar experience is *The God That Failed: Six Studies in Communism* (1950). Again, the gap between the recollected past and the date of publication is significant: by 1950 the Cold War was a feature of the international situation and works such as Orwell's *Animal Farm* (1945) and *Nineteen Eighty-Four* (1949) had marked the fundamental change in attitudes.

Introducing *The God That Failed*, the Labour politician, Richard Crossman, described the phenomenon of conversion and recantation to which the contributors to the book testify:

> It so happens that, in the years between the October revolution and the Stalin–Hitler Pact, numberless men

> of letters, both in Europe and America, were attracted to Communism. They were not 'typical' converts. Indeed, being people of quite unusual sensitivity, they made most abnormal Communists, just as the literary Catholic is a most abnormal Catholic. They had a heightened perception of the spirit of the age, and felt more acutely than others both its frustrations and its hopes. Their conversion therefore expressed, in an acute and sometimes in a hysterical form, feelings which were dimly shared by the inarticulate millions who felt that Russia was 'on the side of the workers.' The intellectual in politics is always 'unbalanced' in the estimation of his colleagues. He peers round the next corner while they keep their eyes on the road; and he risks his faith on unrealized ideas, instead of confining it prudently to humdrum loyalties. He is 'in advance,' and, in this sense, an extremist. If history justifies his premonitions, well and good. But if, on the contrary, history takes the other turning, he must either march forward into the dead end, or ignominiously turn back, repudiating ideas which have become part of his personality.
>
> *The God That Failed* (1950), p.8.

One of the contributors, Arthur Koestler, places his individual experience in the context of a whole generation:

> I was ripe to be converted as a result of my personal case-history; thousands of other members of the intelligentsia and the middle classes of my generation were ripe for it by virtue of other personal case-histories; but however much these differed from case to case, they had a common denominator: the rapid disintegration of moral values, of the pre-1914 pattern of life in post-war Europe, and the simultaneous lure of the new revelation which had come from the East.
>
> I joined the Party (which to this day has remained 'the' Party for all of us who once belonged to it) in 1931, at the beginning of that short-lived period of

> optimism, of that abortive spiritual renaissance, later known as the Pink Decade. The stars of that treacherous dawn were Barbusse, Romain Rolland, Gide and Malraux in France; Piscator, Becher, Renn, Brecht, Eisler, Saeghers in Germany; Auden, Isherwood, Spender in England; Dos Passos, Upton Sinclair, Steinbeck, in the United States. The cultural atmosphere was saturated with Progressive Writers' congresses, experimental theatres, committees for Peace and against Fascism, societies for cultural relations with the U.S.S.R., Russian films and *avant-garde* magazines. It looked indeed as if the Western world, convulsed by the aftermath of war, scourged by inflation, depression, unemployment and the absence of a faith to live for, was at last going to 'clear from the head the masses of impressive rubbish; – Rally the lost and trembling forces of the will – Gather them up and let them loose upon the earth – Till they construct at last a human justice. (Auden.) The new star of Bethlehem had risen in the East; and for a modest sum, Intourist [official Soviet tour agency] was prepared to allow you a short and well-focused glimpse of the Promised Land.
>
> Ibid. p.30.

Earlier, in his novel *Darkness at Noon* (originally written in German; English translation published 1940), Koestler had depicted the passionate idealism motivating some adherents of Communism:

> 'The Party can never be mistaken,' said Rubashov. 'You and I can make a mistake. Not the Party. The Party, comrade, is more than you and I and a thousand others like you and I. The Party is the embodiment of the revolutionary idea in history. History knows no scruples and no hesitation. Inert and unerring, she flows towards her goal. At every bend in her course she leaves the mud which she carries and the corpses of the drowned. History knows her way. She makes

no mistakes. He who has not absolute faith in History does not belong in the Party's ranks.'

Trans. Daphne Hardy (New York: Macmillan, 1941), pp.43–4.

In his contribution to *The God That Failed* Stephen Spender describes a believer of this kind and comments on the 'elements of mysticism' in such a faith that made it attractive to western intellectuals:

He combined a belief in the inexorable Marxist development of history with mystical confidence in the workers. He believed that the workers represented the future, and that given the opportunity, they would flower into a better civilization. Doubtless, if he ever had misgivings about Communist methods, he reflected that, in a workers' world, the classless proletarian society would grow in the soil ploughed over by the methods of the dictatorship of the proletariat.

It is obvious that there were elements of mysticism in this faith. Indeed, I think that this is an attraction of Communism for the intellectual. To believe in political action and economic forces which will release new energies in the world is a release of energy in oneself. One ceases to be inhibited by pity for the victims of revolution. Indeed one can regard pity as a projection of one's own reactionary wish to evade the issue of revolution. One can retain one's faith in the ultimate goals of humanity and at the same time ignore the thousands of people in prison camps, the tens of thousands of slave workers. Do these exist? Whether or not they do, it is bourgeois propaganda to maintain so. Therefore one must deny that there are any slave camps in Russia. These lives have become abstractions in an argument in which the present is the struggle, and the future is Communism – a world where everyone will, eventually, be free. If one admits to oneself the existence of the prison camps one can view them as inevitable sacrifices demanded by the good

1. A Wigan street scene during the Depression.

2. The Jarrow marchers passing through a Bedfordshire village (26 October 1936).

ADOLF IN THE LOOKING-GLASS.

HERR HITLER. "HOW FRIGHTFUL I LOOK TO-DAY!"

3. A Punch Cartoon, 5 December 1934: 'Adolf in the looking-glass. Herr Hitler ''How Frightful I look to-day!''' by Bernard Partridge (1861–1945).

THE MASTER-SINGER OF NUREMBERG

4. A Punch Cartoon, 7 September 1938: 'The Master-Singer of Nuremberg' by Bernard Partridge (1861–1945).

5. Neville Chamberlain on his return from Munich, 30 September 1938.

6. Christopher Isherwood and W.H. Auden about to leave for China (January 1938).

7. George Orwell.

8. Evelyn Waugh.

> cause. It is 'humanitarian' weakness to think too much about the victims. The point is to fix one's eyes on the goal, and then one is freed from the horror and anxiety – quite useless in any case – which inhibit the energies of the Liberal mind.
>
> *The God That Failed* (1950), p.238.

Spender's further comments indicate that a sense of guilt arising from consciousness of their own privileged backgrounds was one of the causes that led intellectuals like himself to espouse Communism (though Spender himself was a member of the Party for only a very short time):

> Moreover, if Communism produces victims, capitalism produces far more. What are the millions of unemployed in peace-time, the millions killed in wars, but the victims of capitalist competition? Capitalism is a system based on victimization in which the number of victims increases all the time. Communism is a system in which, theoretically – when all are Communists in a classless society – there will be no victims. Its victims to-day are the victims not of Communism but of revolution. When the revolution has succeeded and when the dictatorship of the proletariat has 'withered away,' there will be a decreasing number of victims. For Communism does not need exploited classes of people. It needs only co-operation of all men to make a better world. During the early years of the 1930's I used to argue with myself in this way. My arguments were reinforced by feelings of guilt and suspicion that the side of me which pitied the victims of revolution secretly supported the ills of capitalism from which I myself benefited.
>
> Ibid. pp.238–9.

To those who came to maturity in the inter-war years, Soviet Communism seemed to offer a faith that, as some of the vocabulary of the above extracts suggests, was quasi-religious in nature.

During these years Britain was still the mother country for

an Empire largely created during the nineteenth century; and one facet of the left-wing sympathies of the period was a rejection of colonial and imperial policies and attitudes. Towards the end of 1922 Orwell went to Burma, which since 1885 had been under British rule, and spent several years serving in the Indian Imperial Police. Later he wrote in *The Road to Wigan Pier* that after leaving Burma he was

> conscious of an immense weight of guilt that I had got to expiate. I suppose that sounds exaggerated; but if you do for five years a job that you thoroughly disapprove of, you will probably feel the same. I had reduced everything to the simple theory that the oppressed are always right and the oppressors are always wrong; a mistaken theory, but the natural result of being one of the oppressors yourself. I felt that I had got to escape not merely from imperialism but from every form of man's dominion over man. I wanted to submerge myself, to get right down among the oppressed, to be one of them and on their side against their tyrants.

This impulse to 'submerge' himself resulted, as we have seen in an earlier chapter, in his exploration of the life of the poor in the north of England. More directly, the 'expiation' of his guilt produced a number of writings in which he attacked the principles and practice of imperialism.

The essays 'Shooting an Elephant' and 'A Hanging' are short and highly effective examples of Orwell's method, in which what appears to be an objective reporting style is in fact didactic, rhetorical and propagandist. For many of his generation the immensely popular Kipling, who died in 1936, was the chronicler and celebrant of British imperialism, and in his essay 'Rudyard Kipling' (1942) – prompted by a selection from Kipling's verse edited by T.S. Eliot, whose right-wing convictions were well known – Orwell attacks those who fall into the 'error of defending [Kipling] where he is not defensible':

> It is no use pretending that Kipling's view of life, as a whole, can be accepted or even forgiven by any

> civilized person. It is no use claiming, for instance, that when Kipling describes a British soldier beating a 'nigger' with a cleaning rod in order to get money out of him, he is acting merely as a reporter and does not necessarily approve what he describes. There is not the slightest sign anywhere in Kipling's work that he disapproves of that kind of conduct – on the contrary, there is a definite strain of sadism in him, over and above the brutality which a writer of that type has to have. Kipling *is* a jingo imperialist, he *is* morally insensitive and aesthetically disgusting.
>
> *The Collected Essays, Journalism and Letters of George Orwell*, ed. Sonia Orwell and Ian Angus, (1968), p.184.

But the most substantial product of Orwell's time in the East is his novel *Burmese Days* (USA pub. 1934; UK pub. 1935), of which Orwell himself wrote that 'much of it is simply reporting of what I have seen', and which has been described as

> a valuable historical document, although in the guise of a novel, for it recorded vividly the tensions that prevailed in Burma, and the mutual suspicion, despair and disgust that crept into Anglo-Burmese relations as a direct result of the Government of India Act [of 1919] leaving out Burma from the course of its reforms.
>
> Maung Htin Aung, 'George Orwell and Burma', *The World of George Orwell*, ed. Miriam Gross (1971), p.20.

Flory, the protagonist of *Burmese Days*, is an Englishman whose situation and sentiments are very much Orwell's own:

> What was at the centre of all his thoughts now, and what poisoned everything, was the ever bitterer hatred of the atmosphere of imperialism in which he lived. For . . . he had grasped the truth about the English and their Empire. The Indian Empire is a despotism –

> benevolent, no doubt, but still a despotism with theft as its final object.
>
> *Burmese Days* (Secker and Warburg edn, 1971), p.68.

By a paradox that is also expressed in 'Shooting an Elephant' Flory and his fellow officials are both agents of despotism and themselves the victims and prisoners of a tyrannical system which leaves them without individual freedom or self-determination:

> And as to the English of the East, the *sahiblog*, Flory had come so to hate them from living in their society, that he was quite incapable of being fair to them. For after all, the poor devils are no worse than anybody else. They lead unenviable lives; it is a poor bargain to spend thirty years, ill-paid, in an alien country, and then come home with a wrecked liver and a pine-apple backside from sitting in cane chairs, to settle down as the bore of some second-rate Club. On the other hand, the *sahiblog* are not to be idealized. There is a prevalent idea that the men at the 'outposts of Empire' are at least able and hardworking. It is a delusion. Outside the scientific services – the Forest Department, the Public Works Department and the like – there is no particular need for a British official in India to do his job competently. Few of them work as hard or as intelligently as the post-master of a provinicial town in England. The real work of administration is done mainly by native subordinates; and the real backbone of the despotism is not the officials but the Army. Given the Army, the officials and the business-men can rub along safely enough even if they are fools. And most of them *are* fools. A dull, decent people, cherishing and fortifying their dullness behind a quarter of a million bayonets.
>
> *Burmese Days* (Secker and Warburg edn, 1971), pp.68–9.

With a passion and bitterness that derive from both intellectual conviction and personal experience, Orwell condemns the colonial ethos as 'a stifling, stultifying world in which to live.' It is

> a world in which every word and every thought is censored. In England it is hard even to imagine such an atmosphere. Everyone is free in England; we sell our souls in public and buy them back in private, among our friends. But even friendship can hardly exist when every white man is a cog in the wheels of despotism. Free speech is unthinkable. All other kinds of freedom are permitted. You are free to be a drunkard, an idler, a coward, a backbiter, a fornicator; but you are not free to think for yourself. Your opinion on every subject of any conceivable importance is dictated for you by the pukka sahibs' code.
>
> In the end the secrecy of your revolt poisons you like a secret disease. Your whole life is a life of lies. Year after year you sit in Kipling-haunted little Clubs, whisky to right of you, *Pink'un* to left of you, listening and eagerly agreeing while Colonel Bodger develops his theory that these bloody Nationalists should be boiled in oil. You hear your Oriental friends called 'greasy little babus', and you admit, dutifully, that they *are* greasy little babus. You see louts fresh from school kicking grey-haired servants. The time comes when you burn with hatred of your own countrymen, when you long for a native rising to drown their Empire in blood. And in this there is nothing honourable, hardly even any sincerity. For, *au fond*, what do you care if the Indian Empire is a despotism, if Indians are bullied and exploited? You only care because the right of free speech is denied you. You are a creature of the despotism, a pukka sahib, tied tighter than a monk or a savage by an unbreakable system of tabus.
>
> Ibid. pp.65–6.

In an ironic vein that may owe something to E. M. Forster's *A Passage to India* a decade earlier, Orwell depicts the conversation of an Anglo-Indian group. A *memsahib* is complaining that they ' "seem to have no *authority* over the natives nowadays, with all these dreadful Reforms. . . . In some ways they are getting almost as bad as the lower classes at home" ':

> 'Oh, hardly as bad as that, I trust. Still, I am afraid there is no doubt that the democratic spirit is creeping in, even here.'
>
> 'And such a short time ago, even just before the war, they were so *nice* and respectful! The way they salaamed when you passed them on the road – it was really quite charming. I remember when we paid our butler only twelve rupees a month, and really that man loved us like a dog. And now they are demanding forty and fifty rupees, and I find that the only way I can even *keep* a servant is to pay their wages several months in arrears.'
>
> 'The old type of servant is disappearing,' agreed Mr Macgregor. 'In my young days, when one's butler was disrespectful, one sent him along to the jail with a chit saying "Please give the bearer fifteen lashes". Ah well, *eheu fugaces*! Those days are gone for ever, I am afraid.'
>
> 'Ah, you're about right there,' said Westfield in his gloomy way. 'This country'll never be fit to live in again. British Raj is finished if you ask me. Lost Dominion and all that. Time we cleared out of it.'
>
> Whereat there was a murmur of agreement from everyone in the room, even from Flory, notoriously a Bolshie in his opinions, even from young Maxwell, who had been barely three years in the country.
>
> Ibid. p.28.

Right-wing extremism was also part of the political scene in England in the Thirties and is particularly associated with the name of Sir Oswald Mosley (1896–1980). Mosley, a wealthy baronet who was successively a Conservative, Independent and Labour MP and a member of the Labour Government of 1929, founded the British Union of Fascists in 1932, quickly attracted supporters, both individual and corporate, and within a short time was holding mass rallies and disturbing law and order:

> The British Union of Fascists attracted diverse elements including romantically-minded white collar workers and semi-literate toughs in search of excitement. Its leadership was predominantly middle class with a high proportion of ex-army officers. Within eighteen months of its formation it was claiming a membership of twenty thousand. Members were fitted out with black shirts, drilled and paraded and transported to meetings all over the country. A big building in the Kings Road, Chelsea was converted into a blackshirt barracks.
>
> It was clear that the movement had ample funds. Lord Rothermere gave it his backing, which meant the backing of the *Daily Mail*, with its one and a half million circulation, as well as the *Evening News* and the *Sunday Dispatch*. 'Each week the *Sunday Dispatch* is presenting five £1 prizes to readers who send in postcards on "Why I like the Blackshirts" ', it announced. Every effort was made to enlist support among the best people. The *Tatler* published a full page photograph of Mosley with the caption 'We Stopped, and We Looked, and We Listened,' paying tribute to Mosley's 'rare gift of political courage'.
>
> The motives of Mosley's rich backers were not hard to understand. It was a time of uncertainty in which the old values seemed to be crumbling, and with them, perhaps, the very foundations of the established order. The General Strike in 1926 had given a glimpse of the chasm which might one day open; the Invergordon mutiny another. Communists were increasing their following among the unemployed, while the universities appeared to be riddled with pacifism. But Mosley countered ideas of international working-class brotherhood with the slogan 'Britain First': he answered pacifism with a sturdy pride in one's country; he offered to replace ineptitude and vacillation in high

> places with decision and authority. Yet he offered no threat to private property, but stressed that in his corporate state 'individual enterprise and the making of profit are not only permitted, but encouraged'. Fascism, it was argued, had done much for Italy under Mussolini, where it had created a sense of unity between previously warring classes, had fostered ideals of service and obedience in place of the earlier unrest.
>
> Branson and Heinemann, *Britain in the Nineteen Thirties* (1971), pp.282–3.

Mosley took Hitler and Mussolini as his models, but of course they were still relatively little known in England, just as the word 'Fascist' itself had not yet acquired the associations now inseparable from it. A mass meeting in London on 7 June 1934 resulted in violence that went unrestrained by the 760 police on duty there; and a similar failure on the part of the authorities marked a rally and march on 4 October 1936, by which time the anti-semitism of Mosley and his followers had become well known. The Government found it necessary to pass a Public Order Act to empower the police to ban political processions.

As Valentine Cunningham has recently shown in his long and densely documented study of the decade, *British Writers of the Thirties* (1988), some were attracted by 'the impressive toughness and bigness of Fascists and Fascism', with their cult of physical development, fitness and fresh air, and their addiction to mass rallies. Mussolini 'had himself photographed heroically posed in the saddles of horses and motorbikes and in the cockpits of aeroplanes' and was 'widely bruited as being physically hardened and fit', while a contemporary biographer of Mosley, A. K. Chesterton in *Oswald Mosley: Portrait of a Leader* (1936), claimed similar qualities for his subject – as, in Cunningham's words, 'the heroic Olympic swordsman, soldier, airman, fist-fighter . . . the one who can stem Britain's enfeebled modern decline' (p.182). The 1936 Olympic Games, held in Berlin, simultaneously celebrated this aspect of the Fascist and Nazi movements and exemplified their use of mass meetings and propaganda. One of Hitler's

Nuremberg rallies is described in *Goodbye West Country* (1937) by the British writer Henry Williamson (1895–1977), best known for his nature stories such as *Tarka the Otter* (1927) and *Salar the Salmon* (1935), who became an admirer of Hitler and Mosley. In his foreword to *The Flax of Dreams* (1936) Williamson refers to Hitler as 'the great man across the Rhine, whose life symbol is the happy child'. With hindsight it is easy enough to be astonished, as Cunningham is, by the enthusiasm felt for Hitler by a man as thoughtful as Williamson and by the particular grounds for his enthusiasm: 'It was part, astonishingly, of Hitler's attraction for Henry Williamson that he judged the dictator . . . to have eradicated the "crowd hysteria" and "mass panic" of Weimar Germany, astonishing not least because one of *Goodbye West Country's* most rhapsodic peaks is Williamson's attendance at a Nürnberg Parteitag [Party Day]. . .' (Cunningham, op. cit., pp.275–6).

But events of this kind also provoked a reaction against zealotry and violence, and the pacifist movement gained strength in Britain in the middle years of the decade:

> In October 1934, Canon 'Dick' Sheppard* invited men who cared for peace to send him a postcard. The card was to say: 'I renounce war, and I will never support or sanction another.' Why should such an invitation be resisted? To what, after all, did it commit you beyond the act of posting a card? Within a year 80 000 people had renounced war, and the Peace Pledge Union had been founded by those who had signed a pledge which, when war came, was honoured no more than are most temperance pledges. Most of those who joined the Peace Pledge Union, however, did so in the belief that if they gathered enough members war would become impossible. There could be no doubt that the movement was an enormous success. It was given impetus by the Peace Ballot, undertaken originally by the League of Nations Union.

*H.R.L. ('Dick') Sheppard (1880–1937), popular Anglican preacher and ardent pacifist, founded the Peace Pledge Union in 1936.

> Peace Weeks were held, a journal called *Peace News* appeared, big demonstrations in favour of peace through negotiation took place in most unlikely spots. Two thousand people took part in a peace march through Bury, the Rex Cinema in Norbury was packed tight with an audience of 1600, while crowds clamoured for admission at the doors. In November 1937, the Peace Pledge Union had 133 000 members organized into 725 groups, and when two young men were sacked by a firm of Lloyd's underwriters for wearing white as well as red poppies on Armistice Day, the *News Chronicle* sounded a warning: 'The firm's attitude savours of Fascism.'
>
> Julian Symons, *The Thirties: A Dream Revolved* (1975) p.48.

A fictional echo of the period occurs in Evelyn Waugh's story 'An Englishman's Home' (1939), included in his volume *Work Suspended* (1948), in which a middle-class village lady 'at the time of the Peace Ballot . . . had canvassed every cottage in bicycling distance. . . .' A paragraph from the same story that concludes with a sly reference to the Left Book Club reminds us that even at a time of political crisis and agitation not everyone is caught up in the issues of the day:

> Under their stone-tiled roofs the villagers derived substantial comfort from all these aliens. Foreign visitors impressed by the charges of London restaurants and the splendour of the more accessible ducal palaces often express wonder at the wealth of England. A half has not been told them. It is in remote hamlets like Much Malcock that the great reservoirs of national wealth seep back to the soil. The villagers had their Memorial Hall and their club. In the rafters of their church the death-watch beetle had been expensively exterminated for them; their scouts had a bell tent and silver bugles; the district nurse drove her own car; at Christmas their children were surfeited with trees and parties and the cottagers loaded with hampers; if one

> of them was indisposed port and soup and grapes and tickets for the seaside arrived in profusion; at evening their menfolk returned from work laden with perquisites, and all the year round they feasted on forced vegetables. The vicar found it impossible to interest them in the Left Book Club.
>
> *Work Suspended* (1948), p.63.

Even when due allowance has been made for Waugh's comic and satiric purposes, there is surely a good deal of truth in this. At the same time, just as there were many whose ideas were shaped by the Left Book Club, there were others whose pacifist convictions were deeply held. As the decade wore on, however, it became more difficult to see pacifism as an adequate response to the menace represented by Nazism. The mathematician and philosopher Bertrand Russell (1872–1970) relates in his autobiography that, although he decided in the mid-Thirties 'to write a book on the daily increasing menace of war . . . and maintained in it the pacifist position that I had taken up during the First [World] War', he came to realise that his long-held convictions were no longer sound in the changed conditions of the world:

> This attitude, however, had become unconsciously insincere. I had been able to view with reluctant acquiescence the possibility of the supremacy of the Kaiser's Germany; I thought that, although this would be an evil, it would not be so great an evil as a world war and its aftermath. But Hitler's Germany was a different matter. I found the Nazis utterly revolting – cruel, bigoted, and stupid. Morally and intellectually they were alike odious to me. Although I clung to my pacifist convictions, I did so with increasing difficulty. When, in 1940, England was threatened with invasion, I realised that, throughout the First War, I had never seriously envisaged the possibility of utter defeat. I found this possibility unbearable, and at last consciously and definitely decided that I must support what was necessary for victory in the Second War,

however difficult victory might be to achieve, and however painful in its consequences.

This was the last stage in the slow abandonment of many of the beliefs that had come to me in the moment of 'conversion' in 1901. I had never been a complete adherent of the doctrine of non-resistance; I had always recognised the necessity of the police and the criminal law, and even during the First War I had maintained publicly that some wars are justifiable. But I had allowed a larger sphere to the method of non-resistance – or, rather, non-violent resistance – than later experience seemed to warrant. It certainly has an important sphere; as against the British in India, Gandhi led it to triumph. But it depends upon the existence of certain virtues in those against whom it is employed. When Indians lay down on railways, and challenged the authorities to crush them under trains, the British found such cruelty intolerable. But the Nazis had no scruples in analogous situations. The doctrine which Tolstoy preached with great persuasive force, that the holders of power could be morally regenerated if met by non-resistance, was obviously untrue in Germany after 1933. Clearly Tolstoy was right only when the holders of power were not ruthless beyond a point, and clearly the Nazis went beyond this point.

The Autobiography of Bertrand Russell, Volume II: *1914–1944* (1968), pp.191–2.

We have looked so far at a variety of responses – communist, fascist, pacifist – to the problems of the age; but, as the extract from Waugh's story suggests, it would be a mistake to suppose that all those living in England, including the writers of the time, felt an equally strong commitment to one or other ideology or to any ideology at all. We turn next to two writers, Anthony Powell and Waugh himself, who appear – but perhaps only appear – to turn their backs on politics and to find their subject matter in groups and individuals who responded to the pressures of their generation by devoting themselves to a quest for individual fulfilment or pleasure or escape.

The early novels of Anthony Powell (b.1905), like those of Evelyn Waugh, deal mainly with the upper and upper-middle classes; but for all the realism of setting, action and dialogue his aim is not so much sociological analysis as a more far-reaching diagnosis of a spiritual malaise affecting Western civilisation. The hero or anti-hero of his first novel, *Afternoon Men* (1931), is employed, no doubt significantly, in a museum but finds no satisfaction in either his work or his ample leisure: rootless and aimless, he drifts from restaurant to club (those inadequate substitutes for a home or community where one belongs) and from one party to another. The party, with its forced sociability and its opportunities for brief sexual liaisons and temporary escape through alcohol, is one of the upper-class institutions of the period and represents a frenetic quest for pleasure; but the behaviour of the guests is mechanical, they fail to respond to each other in any *human* way, and the social rituals are performed without zest. Conversation is trivial and formulaic and the perception of other people is presented in purely external terms: one of Powell's stylistic mannerisms is to present minor characters as objects whose individuality is reduced to one or two physical features so that one party guest is 'a red-faced man wearing a white tie' and his wife is 'tall and rather splendid in a way, but she was not thin enough, and she had a nose that spoiled her appearance'. 'Appearance' is the keyword: the possibility is not entertained that behind the nose might be a mind and character that compensated for its shortcomings.

In the world of the 'afternoon men' even lust and love have become insipid and mechanical, and there is in Chapter 9 a seduction scene that brings to mind a somewhat similar scene in Eliot's *The Waste Land*:

> Slowly, but very deliberately, the brooding edifice of seduction, creaking and incongruous, came into being, a vast Heath Robinson mechanism, dually controlled by them and lumbering gloomily down vistas of triteness. With a sort of heavy-fisted dexterity the mutually adapted emotions of each of them became

> synchronised, until the unavoidable anti-climax was at hand. Later they dined at a restaurant quite near the flat.

A phrase like 'vistas of triteness' rejects the whole tradition of romantic love and of sexual experience as profound and satisfying: for this couple it ends only in 'anti-climax'. The paradox of Powell's world is that, single-mindedly dedicated to the pursuit of pleasure, his characters find only tedium and emptiness. His theme is the failure of hedonism.

At one point in *Afternoon Men* Atwater is momentarily brought up against the idea of moral responsibility. At a house-party in a Sussex cottage at which he is a guest, the host is mistakenly believed to have gone off and drowned himself. When a woman asks Atwater ' "Do you think it was my fault?" ' his reaction is revealing: 'He felt suddenly as if he were going to be sick. All he wanted was to leave at once before he followed Pringle into the sea'. The moral dimension of life is something he is incapable of confronting, and his suicidal instinct lays bare the nullity of his own existence.

In Powell's second novel, *Venusberg* (1932), the scene is no longer English but international. Lushington, who has much in common with Atwater, is employed by a mass-circulation newspaper and is sent as foreign correspondent to a small Baltic state whose frontiers were re-drawn by the Treaty of Versailles at the end of the Great War. There he finds himself in a world of minor diplomats, exiled aristocrats (both genuine and spurious) and other cosmopolitan figures – a world in which social and political life is superficial and unstable, and sexual relationships are similar. It is in fact the world of *Afternoon Men* writ larger, with its cast drawn from the sad or fraudulent flotsam and jetsam of a Europe that recent history has thrown into confusion.

The epigraph of the novel is a presumably fictitious quotation from Baedeker, the famous series of travel guides that were carried round Europe by well-to-do English tourists in the serene days before 1914:

> Here, according to popular tradition, is situated the

> grotto of Venus, into which she enticed the knight Tannhauser; fine view from the top.

The 'grotto of Venus' and the reminder of Wagner invoke romantic and heroic traditions of love; but the novel that follows presents an ironic contrast between a dead tradition and contemporary life in its sordid and heartless banality. Again, we are inevitably reminded of Eliot's poem of 1922 with its fleeting cosmopolitan figures and its contrasts between a colourful past and a drab present. Even the structure of Powell's novel resembles that of the poem: there is a large number of short chapters with abrupt transitions from one scene to the next, suggesting discontinuity and fragmentation. Powell's style is laconic and his dialogue represents no real communion between individuals. When Lushington lunches with his mistress in Chapter 17, he is worried lest her husband might discover them:

> They sat in one of the cramped wooden partitions into which the room was divided. It was customary to begin the meal with *bouillon*. Ortrud sat next to the wall. Lushington said:
> 'Where does your husband lunch?'
> 'At the Café Weber.'
> 'Every day?'
> 'Yes.'
> 'Does he never come here?'
> 'Of course not.'
> 'Why not?'
> 'Because he always lunches at the Café Weber.'
> Then one day the Professor arrived. They had just finished their *bouillon*. . . .

There are some unobtrusive but telling touches here. The 'cramped' seating, with the married woman trapped against the wall, suggests their lack of freedom; and the *bouillon*, chosen not because they like it but because it is 'customary', forces itself to the foreground of the scene even though it is irrelevant to the central emotional situation – with the effect that the situation seems no more significant or meaningful than the soup.

In Chapter 22 the lovers, whose affair is doomed to be transitory and sterile, visit a baroque palace, now abandoned, that is a relic from a splendid past: 'used at present for nothing in particular', it is 'spoken of as a potential state institution for mental defectives'. The scene seems to externalise the emotional life of the characters:

> Meanwhile it was deserted, though waste paper had been left about on one of the terraces and someone had taken the trouble to overturn and to dismember a colossal imperial statue in bronze which had formerly stood at the end of a vista of trees. Anatomical remains of this were sinking into the turf of the lawn or lying about among the flower beds. The steps of the terrace in front had been broken in places and not yet repaired. From the top of the steps there was a good view of the town, where wisps of smoke hung round the shapeless citadel. . . .
>
> The breeze from the sea blew across the gardens and carried some few remnants of leaves, scraps and odds and ends of twigs across the lawn so that they dashed against the tritons and cornucopia of the fountain. Although snow was lying on the roofs of the town, here it was half melted from the grass. Among the beds without flowers and the chipped cupids, the gnawing of actuality seemed for the moment silenced. In this place which had been left without meaning it seemed easier to feel meaning where there was perhaps none. All was very quiet except for an occasional crackling made now and then as birds flew through the trees, or by the bark or branches of the trees themselves.
>
> 'What shall I do when I have to go away and leave you?'
>
> 'You must not go. I shall come with you. I cannot allow you to go. But why should we talk about that now? Here England is so far away. And you are not

> going to leave me yet. You are not going to leave me yet, are you?'
>
> 'No. Not yet.'
>
> They went up into the woods beyond the garden and along the paths that led inland and upwards, because the palace was in a hollow. The chilly avenues were deserted. Once a peasant passed dragging some wood on a sledge and, with some obscure remembrance of another epoch, touched his cap. The trees swayed about uncertainly. She said:
>
> 'You do love me, don't you?'
>
> 'Yes. I love you.'
>
> 'And I love you?'
>
> 'Yes. You love me.'
>
> They walked on between the birch trees.
>
> 'And now I must go back,' she said.
>
> 'Why?'
>
> 'Domestic duties. You forget that I am a wife. I must go back to my home.'
>
> 'So soon? Can't we stay here for a bit?'
>
> 'No. I must go back.'
>
> They turned down one of the paths which led back towards the sea and brought them to the embankment promenade, a walk that had been fashionable before the Independence. But now that the town had been rebuilt no one came here. Instead the people walked up and down the main boulevard. Only a few soldiers were wandering two-and-two along the embankment, their sheepskin caps and long overcoats making them like the accepted representations of Noah and his children.

The 'good view of the town' recalls the 'fine view' of the novel's epigraph; but it is no 'grotto of Venus' that is available to these modern lovers. Inhabitants of a world torn apart by military action and political and economic chaos, they are unable to find peace and stability in their personal lives or to view their personal futures with confidence. The broken statues in the baroque palace stand not only for a Europe that bears the physical scars of war but for the destruction of a long tradition of European civilisation, including much of what gives coherence and meaning to private lives.

Yet another of Powell's novels of the early Thirties, *From a View to a Death* (1933), suggests the chaos and lunacy that could lie just beneath a decorous, even banal surface. When Major Fosdick is introduced, he seems to be, in spite of some mild and fairly amiable eccentricity, a commonplace and predictable figure, even a stereotype – a retired army officer living in an English village. But as soon as he is alone, a curious 'slippage' occurs; and the reader, previously lulled into a sense of security now seen to be false, has the illusion of looking down into a murky and obscure chasm:

> He went upstairs to his dressing-room and when he had arrived there he locked the door. Then he turned to the bottom drawer of his wardrobe, where he kept all his oldest shooting-suits. He knelt down in front of this and pulled it open. Below the piles of tweed was a piece of brown paper and from under the brown paper he took two parcels tied up with string. Major Fosdick undid the loose knots of the first parcel and took from out of it a large picture-hat that had no doubt been seen at Ascot some twenty years before. The second parcel contained a black sequin evening dress of about the same date. Removing his coat and waist-coat, Major Fosdick slipped the evening dress over his head and, shaking it so that it fell down into position, he went to the looking-glass and put on the hat. When he had it arranged at an angle that was to his satisfaction, he lit his pipe and taking a copy of *Through the Western Highlands with Rod and Gun* from the dressing-table, he sat down. In this costume he read until it was time to change for dinner.
>
> For a good many years now he had found it restful to do this for an hour or two every day when he had the opportunity. He himself would have found it difficult to account for such an eccentricity to anyone whom he might have happened to encounter during one of these periods and it was for this reason that he was accustomed to gratify his whim only at times when there was a reasonable expectation that his

privacy would be respected by his family. Publicly he himself would refer to these temporary retirements from the arena of everyday life as his *Forty Winks*.

From a View to a Death (John Lehmann, 1948), p.22.

Powell's combination of a deadpan style with farce that has disturbing overtones and yet exploits traditional comic incongruity (the pipe-smoking and book-title in relation to the Major's costume) – all this is very characteristic of the period. It suggests both a debt to popularised Freudian psychology (compare Auden's poem of 1929 beginning 'Sir, no man's enemy') and a sense that to live in the Thirties was to dwell, so to speak, in an earthquake zone where the familiar landscape could suddenly be transformed and the ground disappear from under one's feet.

The outstanding chronicler of the period's frantic hedonism and moral and spiritual emptiness was Evelyn Waugh (1903–66). A schoolboy during the war, he had reached manhood in the twenties and had begun his literary career before the end of that decade. As Michael Davie, the editor of Waugh's diaries, has noted, 'On 1 February 1925, hearing of the engagement of two friends, Waugh wrote in his diary: "It makes me sad for them because any sort of happiness or permanence seems so infinitely remote from any one of us" ' (*The Diaries of Evelyn Waugh*, Penguin edn, 1979, p.159). Waugh came from a privileged middle-class background: his father was a well-known publisher and he was sent to a public school and to Oxford, but he shared the malaise of his generation. His response to it was a series of brilliant comic novels that anatomise the manners and values of the English upper-classes at a time when they still enjoyed a lifestyle that became extinct after the Second World War. As he wrote in 1963 in a preface to his novel *Scoop*, which had originally appeared in 1938, much of the world depicted therein is 'anachronistic': 'Younger readers must accept my assurance that such people and their servants did exist quite lately and are not pure fantasy'. In his early novels Waugh also portrays his own generation, the Bright Young People who sought to escape the problems and responsibilities of the age in a frenetic quest for pleasure, or at least temporary oblivion: it was the period of the jazz band, the cocktail, the night club, and above all of the party, as Waugh makes clear in his first novel of the thirties, *Vile Bodies*:

> Masked parties, Savage parties, Victorian parties, Greek parties, Wild West parties, Russian parties, Circus parties, parties where one had to dress as somebody else, almost naked parties in St John's Wood, parties in flats and studios and houses and ships and hotels and night clubs, in windmills and swimming-baths, tea parties at school where one ate muffins and meringues and tinned crab, parties at Oxford where one drank brown sherry and smoked Turkish cigarettes, dull dances in London and comic dances in Scotland and disgusting dances in Paris – all that succession and repetition of massed humanity. . . .
>
> *Vile Bodies*, (Penguin edn, 1958), p.123.

As social history such accounts refer specifically to the period during and immediately following Waugh's time at Oxford in the twenties; but there is a strongly non-realistic element in his work (farce, for instance, is a favourite mode), and they can also be taken as metaphorical or symbolic statements about the English upper-classes, morally adrift and uncertain of the future, in the inter-war years. Even the narrative structure of these novels, which involves the juxtaposition or collage of many short scenes with abrupt cutting from one to another, suggests something of the fragmentary and unsatisfying nature of the experiences recounted; and the dialogue is often laconic and even formulaic, with much use of fashionable slang. The difference between such techniques and those of the more leisurely, expansive and coherent nineteenth-century novel represents the difference between an age of uncertainty and an age of confidence.

The decade began for Waugh with a failure, a success and a commitment. His brief first marriage ended in divorce; his second novel, *Vile Bodies*, was a considerable success; and in September 1930 he was admitted into the Roman Catholic Church. Since he believed at the time that he would never be able to re-marry, he undertook a series of extensive travels that occupied most of the decade, and these are fully reflected in his work. *Remote People* (1931), the outcome of a visit to Abyssinia (Ethiopia) as a journalist to cover the coronation of the Emperor, was the first of his travel books, and he was back there again in 1935 to cover the opening stages of the war between Abyssinia and Italy, and yet again in the following year, *Waugh in Abyssinia* being the outcome of these visits. (Waugh's own later selections from these travel books are contained in the volume *When the Going was Good*). The interesting thing is that in leaving England so far behind Waugh found confusion and anarchy that were in essence not so very different from what he had discerned in London society: Addis Ababa reminded him of the world of Lewis Carroll ('it is to *Alice in Wonderland* that my thoughts recur in seeking some historical parallel for life in Addis Ababa': *Remote People*, 1931, p.29), and the same world of comic fantasy appears in his English novels (*Alice*, indeed, had provided the epigraph for *Vile Bodies*). It is as if he has carried with him his own perception of a world that has lost any meaning it may have possessed.

His travels in Africa are drawn on in *Black Mischief* (1932) as well as the later *Scoop* (in the preface to the former novel he states that 'The scene . . . was a fanciful confusion of many territories'). The English residents in the fictitious African country depicted in *Black Mischief* are a mixture of fatuous incompetence and seedy self-interest, and there is a comic and ironic distance between what they really are and how they appear to the naively enthusiastic emperor keen to modernise his country. The playboy Basil Seal 'stood for him as the personification of all that glittering, intangible Western culture to which he aspired' (Penguin edn, 1980, p.113); but Western ideals themselves have crumbled, as is made clear when Basil tells the emperor that

> '. . . we've got a much easier job now than we should have had fifty years ago. If we'd had to modernize a country then it would have meant constitutional monarchy, bi-cameral legislature, proportional re-

> presentation, women's suffrage, independent judicature, freedom of the Press, referendums. . .'
> 'What is all that?' asked the Emperor.
> 'Just a few ideas that have ceased to be modern.'
>
> *Black Mischief* (Penguin edn, 1980), p.128.

The books produced by Waugh's other journeyings also contain evidence that he found in distant places universal madness and a confirmation of his own deep pessimism. At the end of 1932, for instance, he went to Brazil, a visit recorded in *92 Days.* In the wilds of British Guiana he came across a religious maniac who inspired a story, 'The Man Who Liked Dickens' (written in February 1933), which itself grew into a full-length novel, *A Handful of Dust*, later described as 'a study of other sorts of savages at home and the civilised man's helpless plight among them'. A 1938 visit to Mexico produced *Robbery under Law*, described as 'notes on anarchy': Waugh found Mexico under its dictatorship a 'waste land, part of a dead or, at any rate, a dying planet', and added significantly that 'There is no distress of theirs to which we might not be equally subject'. Again the seminal influence of T.S. Eliot seems to be behind the phrase 'waste land', and we recall also that *A Handful of Dust*, often considered Waugh's finest novel, takes its title from one of Eliot's poems.

Part of Waugh's achievement in his early fiction was to devise and exploit a form and technique that expressed the spiritual malaise of the age. In particular his experimental use of dialogue dramatises the shallowness and hollowness of the lives led by his characters. Here is the whole of Chapter 11 of *Vile Bodies*:

> Adam rang up Nina.
> 'Darling, I've been so happy about your telegram. Is it really true?'
> 'No, I'm afraid not.'
> 'The Major *is* bogus?'
> 'Yes.'
> 'You haven't got any money?'

'No.'

'We aren't going to be married to-day?'

'No.'

'I see.'

'Well?'

'I said, I see.'

'Is that all?'

'Yes, that's all, Adam.'

'I'm sorry.'

'I'm sorry, too. Good-bye.'

'Good-bye, Nina.'

Later Nina rang up Adam.

'Darling, is that you? I've got something rather awful to tell you.'

'Yes?'

'You'll be furious.'

'Well?'

'I'm engaged to be married.'

'Who to?'

'I hardly think I can tell you.'

'Who?'

'Adam, you won't be beastly about it, will you?'

'Who is it?'

'Ginger.'

'I don't believe it.'

'Well, I am. That's all there is to it.'

'You're going to marry Ginger?'

'Yes.'

'I see.'

'Well?'

'I said, I see.'

'Is that all?'

'Yes, that's all, Nina.'

'When shall I see you?'

'I don't want ever to see you again.'

'I see.'

'Well?'

'I said, I see.'

'Well, good-bye.'

'Good-bye. . . . I'm sorry, Adam.'

The modes of communication adopted by these characters are mechanical, laconic and disembodied: the telephone and the telegram. The subject, decisions about marriage, is one of the most momentous in anyone's life, but the treatment is offhand and banal. The very short sentences, many of them consisting of a single word, indicate absence of feeling and failure of communication. Such indications of feeling as exist are purely formulaic and automatic: 'Darling', 'beastly', 'furious'. Repetition of certain phrases ('I see', 'I'm sorry', 'that's all') intensifies the sense of a form of speech in which no real exchange of ideas or feelings is taking place and no rapport is achieved. The brevity of the utterances means that there is no development or exploration of these important topics: these are characters incapable of other than superficial responses to experience, trapped within the paralysing conventions of their age and class. Physical separation, the telephone reducing them to mere voices, is an outward manifestation of an emotional and spiritual isolation. Finally, the total absence of description or comment indicates the withdrawal of the narrator who might otherwise endow the scene with meaning: the firm narratorial authority of a nineteenth-century novelist such as George Eliot has totally disappeared, and with it a sense of standards being set and clear judgements being made.

For Samuel Hynes *Vile Bodies* is both 'a brilliantly comic novel' and 'a profoundly serious moral document': 'I would not call it satire; it is rather, I think, a surreal or expressionist attempt to record reality at a time when it seemed more and more to be, by any rational observation, unreal' (*The Auden Generation: Literature and Politics in England in the 1930s*, p.63). Hynes also sees Waugh's novel as 'a precursor of later writing of the decade: in its prophecy of war, in its consciousness of the separateness of the younger generation, in its contemptuous hostility to the politics of the establishment, in its irony, in its bitter, farcical wit, and perhaps most importantly in the way Waugh has gone beyond probability and beyond realism to create a parabolic world, a comical Unreal City of sad, yearning Bright Young People.' It is, however, such writers as Auden and Orwell, rather than Waugh, who were to turn out to be most fully representative of what Aldous Huxley in his *Ends and Means* (1937) calls the 'ferocious theologies' of the decade.

3 The Spanish Civil War: 'To-day the struggle'

At Easter 1936 the poet Louis MacNeice visited Spain and found it 'ripe as an egg for revolt and ruin'. The phrase occurs in a section of his long poem 'Autumn Journal' that recounts his travels in that country. An English tourist he comes across offers the opinion that ' "There's going to be trouble shortly in this country" ', and the poem ends with the following lines:

> . . . only an inch behind
>   This map of olive and ilex, this painted hoarding,
> Careless of visitors the people's mind
>   Was tunnelling like a mole to day and danger.
> And the day before we left
>   We saw the mob in flower at Algeciras
> Outside a toothless door, a church bereft
>   Of its images and its aura.
> And at La Linea while
>   The night put miles between us and Gibraltar
> We heard the blood-lust of a drunkard pile
>   His heaven high with curses;
> And next day took the boat
>   For home, forgetting Spain, not realising
> That Spain would soon denote
>   Our grief, our aspirations;
> Not knowing that our blunt
>   Ideals would find their whetstone, that our spirit
> Would find its frontier on the Spanish front,
>   Its body in a rag-tag army.

(*Collected Poems*, p.112)

The closing lines refer to the civil war that was to break out that summer, and specifically to those who went out from

Britain to fight for the 'Ideals' and 'aspirations' that the struggle in Spain seemed to them to embody.

This chapter, which will explore the relationship between events in Spain in 1936–9 and the accounts of those events in prose and verse written by combatants and observers, has begun with a poem and will refer to other poems. But the notion of the Spanish Civil War as a 'poets' war', a conflict in which most of the participants from outside Spain were writers and intellectuals, though once current has long been exposed as misleading. As Valentine Cunningham has shown, although the conflict produced some 'revolutionary art of a high order' and provided 'a situation where the dreams and aspirations of the Thirties generation of critics and writers could be tested' (Introduction to *The Penguin Book of Spanish Civil War Verse*, 1980, p.64), those who fought were actually drawn from a great variety of backgrounds. Of the 2762 Britons who fought with the International Brigade, about four-fifths came from the working class; the first two English volunteers, for instance, were tailors from the East End. Especially remembered are a handful of gifted writers, such as John Cornford, who were killed in Spain, but Cornford was only one of the 543 volunteers who died. The wound in the throat that Orwell received in Spain is celebrated but about 1200 others were wounded, some of them much more seriously than Orwell. Moreover, while some accounts convey the impression that only men went out to fight in Spain, a number of women took part; indeed, the first Briton to be killed was Felicia Browne, a London artist. It was, to be sure, as Cunningham says, extraordinary that so many foreign writers (from France, the USA, and elsewhere as well as Britain, it should be noted) felt impelled to go to Spain: 'What was startling and special about Spain was that this relatively small-scale war had so many voluntary writer-participants in it – whether they were doing medical work or actually fighting, were engaged in propaganda or political activities, or had gone to Spain simply to report events.' But the Civil War was, after all, a struggle of the Spanish people, aided by a large number of foreigners who for the most part were not writers. Inevitably, however, as with the First World War, it is mainly the writers who have given us the most memorable accounts of what happened; and it is on them that this chapter will draw heavily.

The war began on 18 July 1936 with the revolt of a group of Spanish generals as an expression of their discontent with the left-wing anti-clerical coalition government that had been elected earlier in the year. Civilians were quickly armed and the conflict spread throughout Spain, of which parts were held by the rebels or 'nationalists' and parts by the government or 'republicans'. Other countries soon became involved by sending supplies and personnel: Soviet Russia, for instance, supported the government, while Nazi Germany and Fascist Italy supported General Franco and his forces. The International Brigade was formed to fight for the elected government in its struggle against an enemy that was identified with Fascism. After three years of bitter fighting, during which about three-quarters of a million lives were lost (both combatants and civilians), Franco was victorious and established himself as dictator.

The participation of foreign powers and the involvement of individuals from Britain and elsewhere transformed a civil war, as A.J.P. Taylor has said, into 'a great international question'. Although Britain, France and other countries refused to intervene, the danger of escalation into a European or world war was a real one. As we shall see, the issues were complex, and not everyone in Britain supported the same side. The significant point for the moment is that Spain was, to quote Taylor again, 'transformed into the battleground of rival ideologies', where issues that for many British intellectuals had until that time been theoretical or remote became actualised. Spain thus became a testing-ground of doctrines and convictions, a summons to translate ideas into action. As Valentine Cunningham says in *British Writers of the Thirties*, 'If there is one decisive event which focuses the hopes and fears of the literary '30s, a moment that seems to summarize and test the period's myths and dreams, to enact and encapsulate its dominant themes and images, the Spanish Civil War is it' (p.419).

Some, of course, held convictions without feeling the necessity, or having the opportunity, to translate them into action. In *Authors Take Sides on the Spanish War* (1937) the responses of a large number of intellectuals were given to the following questions:

> Are you for, or against, the legal Government and the People of Republican Spain?
>
> Are you for, or against, Franco and Fascism?

The introduction claimed that 'it is impossible any longer to take no side'. As might be expected, the replies have much in common, and the following brief selection of those made by some of the more notable figures of the period will indicate the general trend:

> W.H. Auden
>
> I support the Valencia Government in Spain because its defeat by the forces of International Fascism would be a major disaster for Europe. It would make a European war more probable; and the spread of Fascist Ideology and practice to countries as yet comparatively free from them, which would inevitably follow upon a Fascist victory in Spain, would create an atmosphere in which the creative artist and all who care for justice, liberty and culture would find it impossible to work or even exist.
>
> C. Day Lewis
>
> The struggle in Spain is part of a conflict going on now all over the world. I look upon it quite simply as a battle between light and darkness, of which only a blind man could be unaware. Both as a writer and as a member of the Communist Party I am bound to help in the fight against Fascism, which means certain destruction or living death for humanity.
>
> Louis MacNeice
>
> I support the Valencia Government in Spain. Normally I would only support a cause because I hoped to get something out of it. Here the reason is stronger; if

> this cause is lost, nobody with civilised values may be able to get anything out of anything.

Some responses were more banal, and some more rhetorical, than those quoted. The chorus was not quite unanimous: Evelyn Waugh, for example, declared 'If I were a Spaniard I should be fighting for General Franco', but that as an Englishman he was 'not in the predicament of choosing between two evils' (p.57), and T.S. Eliot wrote more cautiously:

> While I am naturally sympathetic, I still feel convinced that it is best that at least a few men of letters should remain isolated, and take no part in these collective activities.
>
> Ibid. p.56.

Ezra Pound expressed similar sentiments in different terms: 'Spain is an emotional luxury to a gang of sap-headed dilettantes' (p.57), and Orwell himself, who did not contribute to the symposium, wrote in a letter to Stephen Spender (2 April 1938) of 'that damned rubbish of signing manifestos to say how wicked it all is', while Graham Greene referred to 'the sweeping statements, the safe marble gestures, the self-importance – "I stand with the People and Government of Spain" '. As these brief excerpts show, some were suspicious of, or exasperated by, verbal expressions of solidarity, and in any case not all saw the issues as clear-cut or involving an unqualified opposition of right and wrong; but it remains true that most of the younger generation of writers were strongly anti-Franco.

It was a generation that responded, in many cases with deeds as well as words, to the summons to take sides. As Auden wrote in his 'Spain 1937', which was to become the most famous poem to be produced by the Spanish Civil War:

> Many have heard it on remote peninsulas,
> On sleepy plains, in the aberrant fisherman's islands
> Or the corrupt heart of the city,
> Have heard and migrated like gulls or the seeds of a flower.

They clung like burrs to the long expresses that lurch
Through the unjust lands, through the night, through the alpine tunnel;
They floated over the oceans;
They walked the passes. All presented their lives.

On that arid square, that fragment nipped off from hot
Africa, soldered so crudely to inventive Europe;
On that tableland scored by rivers,
Our thoughts have bodies; the menacing shapes of our fever

Are precise and alive. For the fears which made us respond
To the medicine ad. and the brochure of winter cruises
Have become invading battalions;
And our faces, the institute-face, the chain-store, the ruin

Are projecting their greed as the firing squad and the bomb.
Madrid is the heart. Our moments of tenderness blossom
As the ambulance and the sandbag;
Our hours of friendship into a people's army.

The English Auden, pp.211–12.

The phrase 'to-day the struggle' recurs throughout Auden's poem, and he sees the struggle as representing for British intellectuals a 'choice' and a 'decision', requiring them to examine their beliefs and their consciences as the French Revolution had required those of Wordsworth's generation to do. Auden conveys a strong sense of living at a crisis in history, with the exhilaration as well as the responsibility and uncertainty of that situation; and the note of idealism, of participation in the birth of a new world, is strong in much of the writing of this period.

'On Guard for Spain!', a poem by the Marxist writer Jack Lindsay, demands rhetorically:

> Have you ever come out of the tangled undergrowth
> Into the clearing of history?
> Then you have lived in Spain,
> Spain of these years of pang and aspiration,
> Spain the arena where a weaponless man
> takes the charge of a bull of havoc,
> Spain where the workers, going to battle,
> go as to a fiesta,
> Spain.
> Salute to Spain!
>
> *Left Review*, III (March 1937) p.79.

Significantly, the word 'history' is prominent in the writings that were generated by contemporary events during these years. It reappears in a poem, 'Full Moon at Tierz: Before the Storming of Huesca', by John Cornford (1915–36):

> The past, a glacier, gripped the mountain wall,
> And time was inches, dark was all,
> But here it scales the end of the range,
> The dialectic's point of change,
> Crashes in light and minutes to its fall.
>
> Time present is a cataract whose force
> Breaks down the banks even at its source,
> And history forming in our hands
> Not plasticene but roaring sands,
> Yet we must swing it to its final course. . . .
>
> *Collected Writings* (1986), p.38.

Spain is seen as a country transformed, a melting-pot for the creation of a new kind of society. Auden wrote in the *New Statesman & Nation* on 30 January 1937 – that is, while the war was in its early stages – that

> . . . a revolution is really taking place, not an odd

> shuffle or two in cabinet appointments. In the last six months [the Spanish] people have been learning what it is to inherit their own country, and once a man has tasted freedom he will not lightly give it up; freedom to choose for himself and to organise his life, freedom not to depend for good fortune on a clever and outrageous piece of overcharging or a windfall of drunken charity. That is why, only eight hours away at the gates of Madrid where this wish to live has no possible alternative expression than the power to kill, General Franco has already lost two professional armies and is in the process of losing a third.

Orwell, arriving in Barcelona in December 1936, found a city in which socialist ideals were suddenly translated into reality:

> . . . when one came straight from England the aspect of Barcelona was something startling and overwhelming. It was the first time that I had ever been in a town where the working class was in the saddle. Practically every building of any size had been seized by the workers and was draped with red flags or with the red and black flag of the Anarchists; every wall was scrawled with the hammer and sickle and with the initials of the revolutionary parties; almost every church had been gutted and its images burnt. Churches here and there were being systematically demolished by gangs of workmen. Every shop and café had an inscription saying that it had been collectivised; even the boot-blacks had been collectivised and their boxes painted red and black. Waiters and shopwalkers looked you in the face and treated you as an equal. Servile and even ceremonial forms of speech had temporarily disappeared. . . . And it was the aspect of the crowds that was the queerest thing of all. In outward appearance it was a town in which the wealthy classes had practically ceased to exist. Except for a small number of women and foreigners there were no 'well-dressed' people at all. Practically everyone wore rough work-

> ing-class clothes, or blue overalls or some variant of the militia uniform. All this was queer and moving. There was much in it that I did not understand, in some ways I did not even like it, but I recognized it immediately as a state of affairs worth fighting for.
>
> *Homage to Catalonia* (Penguin edition, 1977), pp.8–9.

Such accounts recall Wordsworth's famous lines on the French Revolution:

> Bliss was it in that dawn to be alive,
> But to be young was very heaven!

But these lines were first published in 1809, twenty years after the event, in a poem titled 'French Revolution, as it Appeared to Enthusiasts', and there is something of the same revisionary retrospect in Orwell's account, though the perspective of time is much shorter, if one reads the passage in context at the beginning of *Homage to Catalonia.* There Orwell, writing only seven months after the date in question, notes that the period 'has already receded into enormous distance. Later events have obliterated it much more completely than they have obliterated 1935 or 1905, for that matter', and that when he arrived in Spain, even though the revolutionary spirit was exciting to one coming from England, 'To anyone who had been there since the beginning it probably seemed even in December or January that the revolutionary period was ending'.

As these comments suggest, Orwell's enthusiasm gave way to disillusion, or at least a more sober sense of reality. Returning to England after being wounded in action, he wrote in a letter of 31 July 1937:

> My wound was not much, but it was a miracle it did not kill me. The bullet went clean through my neck but missed everything except one vocal cord, or rather the nerve governing it, which is paralysed. At first I had no voice at all, but now the other vocal

> cord is compensating and the damaged one may or may not recover. My voice is practically normal but I can't shout to any extent. I also can't sing, but people tell me this doesn't matter. I am rather glad to have been hit by a bullet because I think it will happen to us all in the near future and I am glad to know that it doesn't hurt to speak of. What I saw in Spain did not make me cynical but it does make me think that the future is pretty grim. It is evident that people can be deceived by the anti-Fascist stuff exactly as they were deceived by the gallant little Belgium stuff, and when war comes they will walk straight into it. I don't, however, agree with the pacifist attitude, as I believe you do. I still think one must fight for Socialism and against Fascism, I mean fight physically with weapons, only it is as well to discover which is which.

But those who were inspired by the revolutionary fervour of 1936 could hardly foresee that such a reaction would set in so soon; and some, of course, did not survive to see the waning of the early belief in simple and clear-cut issues, a struggle between good and evil.

Writing earlier in the war, John Cornford noted – without Orwell's benefit of hindsight – the same profound change:

> In Barcelona one can understand physically what the dictatorship of the proletariat means. All the Fascist press has been taken over. The real rule is in the hands of the militia committees. There is a real terror against the Fascists. But that doesn't alter the fact that the place is free – and conscious all the time of its freedom. Everywhere in the streets are armed workers and militiamen, and sitting in the cafés which used to belong to the bourgeoisie. The huge Hotel Colon overlooking the main square is occupied by the United Socialist Party of Catalonia. Further down, in a huge block opposite the Bank of Spain, is the Anarchist headquarters. The palace of a marquis in the Rambla is a C.P. headquarters. But one does not feel the tension. The mass of the people are oblivious of the

> Anarchist-Government trouble brewing, and simply are enjoying their freedom. The streets are crowded all day, and there are big crowds round the radio palaces. But there is nothing at all like tension or hysteria. It's as if in London the armed workers were dominating the streets – it's obvious that they wouldn't tolerate Mosley or people selling *Action* in the streets. And that wouldn't mean that the town wasn't free in the real sense. It is genuinely a dictatorship of the majority, supported by the overwhelming majority.
>
> *Collected Writings*, p.174.

At a later stage of the war, reviewing a memoir of Cornford (who had died in action, probably on his twenty-first birthday, at the end of 1936), Stephen Spender wrote of him:

> Reading this book, one is discovering the potentialities of a generation. Cornford lived for a form of society for which he was also willing to die. When democracy in Spain was threatened, it was natural for him to fight, and in fighting he felt that he was both defending something real and helping to create something new. His spirit was not a resurrection of 1914.
>
> Cornford is immensely significant not merely because he was young and brave, but because he lived and died with the courage of a purpose which reaches far beyond himself and which effectively challenges the barbarism and defeatism of the age we live in. One may feel, as I do, that the pattern of this young hero is over-simplified; his vision of life is impatient and violent, it leaves too many questions unanswered, he burns out too quickly, rushing headlong to his death; but nevertheless it is a pattern which in other lives may take on a greater richness without losing Cornford's power and determination. The spirit of Cornford and some of his comrades rises like a phoenix from the ashes of Spain, which are the ashes of Europe.
>
> *New Statesman and Nation*, 12 November 1938.

Earlier, Spender himself had written (*Daily Worker*, 19 April 1937):

> The fact is that fundamental change has taken place in the mentality of the Spanish people. No one can talk with older peasants and workers in Spain, and the young, politically-minded people of the Republic, without realizing that a gulf of centuries divides the two generations living in Spain at this moment. Military defeats of the Spanish people there may be, but a conquest of their minds is now impossible, and since that is so, they will eventually win. As Cisneros remarked to me whilst we were looking at a large wall-map of Spain, 'They will never defeat us.' And the extraordinary achievements of the Spanish People's Air Force go far to show that Franco will never win the war.

Spender's final prediction, perhaps slightly evasive as expressed here, was not in the event a sound one, and Franco's victory inaugurated a generation of dictatorship.

Cornford is a figure of considerable interest and in some ways characteristic of his generation. Born in 1915 of a distinguished family of Cambridge intellectuals (his father was a classical scholar, his mother a poet and a descendant of both Wordsworth and Darwin), he joined the Young Communist League, and then at the age of nineteen the Communist Party of Great Britain. Within three weeks of the civil war breaking out in Spain, he left for Barcelona and, as already noted, was killed before the end of the year. When Cornford set out for Spain, his father gave him the pistol he himself had used in the Great War; this was, as Valentine Cunningham notes, a symbolic act, for the events of 1936 represented the first contact of the younger generation, those born too late to remember the experiences of 1914–18, with the realities of war.

In a later stanza of his 'Full Moon at Tierz' Cornford places the struggle in Spain in the context of a wider struggle for freedom that also embraces the unemployed in Britain:

England is silent under the same moon,
From Clydeside to the gutted pits of Wales.
The innocent mask conceals that soon
Here too our freedom's swaying in the scales.
O understand before too late
Freedom was never held without a fight.

In Spain, like many others, he found a practical challenge to his principles and convictions. As he wrote in the letter of August 1936 already quoted from:

> Going into action. Thank God for something to do at last. I shall fight like a Communist if not like a soldier. All my love. Salute. . . .
>
> Up till now this letter has been miserable. For this reason. I came out with the intention of staying a few days, firing a few shots, and then coming home. Sounded fine, but you just can't do things like that. You can't play at civil war, or fight with a reservation you don't mean to get killed. It didn't take long to realise that either I was here in earnest or else I'd better clear out. I tried to avoid the dilemma. Then I felt so lonely and bad I tried to get a pass back to Barcelona. But the question was decided for me. Having joined, I am in whether I like it or not. And I like it. Yesterday we went out to attack, and the prospect of action was terribly exhilarating – hence the message on the top of the page. But in the end we went back without doing anything. But I am settling down, picking up scraps of the language and beginning to feel happy. I think I'll make a good fighter, and I'm glad to be here.
>
> Op. cit., pp.174–5.

And for him and others Spain was a paradigm or model of what would necessarily come elsewhere rather than a special case or isolated problem. As Rex Warner (b.1905) wrote in his poem 'The Tourist Looks at Spain', published in *New Writing* in August 1937:

'It is the aim that is right and the end is freedom.
In Spain the veil is torn.
In Spain is Europe, England also is in Spain.
There the sea recedes and there the mirror is no longer
blurred.'. . .
See Spain and see the world. Freedom extends
or contracts in all hearts.
Near Bilbao are buried the vanguard of our army.
It is us too they defended who defended Madrid.

These lines remind us that the price of the struggle for freedom was a heavy one: and Cornford's poems and letters bear witness to the human cost. His 'A Letter from Aragon' commemorates the death of a comrade:

This is a quiet sector of a quiet front.

We buried Ruiz in a new pine coffin,
But the shroud was too small and his washed feet stuck
out.
The stink of his corpse came through the clean pine
boards
And some of the bearers wrapped handkerchiefs round
their faces.
Death was not dignified. . . .

Collected Writings, p.41.

The right-wing response to intellectuals of the Left such as Orwell and Cornford may be represented by Roy Campbell (1901–57) who, born in South Africa, came to England in 1918 and at the beginning of the decade with which we are concerned published *The Georgiad* (1931), a satirical attack on the Bloomsbury Group. As his autobiographical *Broken Record* (1934) indicates, Campbell espoused Fascism and in the Civil War he fought on Franco's side. His long pro-Fascist poem *Flowering Rifle: A Poem from the Battlefield of Spain* appeared in 1939 and combines the heroic couplets of traditional political satire (as in Dryden and Pope) with a belligerent and loud-voiced rhetoric that is all his own: at the beginning of the poem England is

. . . a Land
Where all the sweet emoluments are thrown
To that snug, sinister, and bungling drone,
The fist-shut Left, so dextrous with the dirk,
The striker, less in battle than from work;
The weed of Life that grows where air is hot
With 'Meetings' for its aspidistra-plot;
That leaves its labour to the hammering tongue
And grows, a cactus, out of hot-house dung;. . .

Flowering Rifle, Part One, 'A Letter from the San Mateo Front', *Collected Poems*, Vol. II (Bodley Head edn, 1957), p.38.

Later Campbell's bludgeoning satire is directed at more specific targets that will be familiar to readers of this book:

Since in a land where everything's called New
That's ready to dilapidate in two –
With 'New Verse' and 'New Statesman' to be new with
Alas, it's a New Newness they could do with!

Ibid. p.44.

Given its general tone and its specific attacks upon named left-wing writers, it is not surprising that Campbell's poem was severely reviewed by Spender in *The New Statesman*, where he described it (11 March 1939) as

> an incoherent, biased, unobjective, highly coloured and distorted account of one man's experiences of the Spanish war, seen through the eyes of a passionate partisan of Franco. . . . It is a kind of three-decker sandwich consisting of one layer of invective against the intellectuals of the Left, the International Brigade, the Spanish Republican Army, etc.; a second layer of autobiography concerning the exploits of Mr Campbell and his flowering rifle; and a top layer of rhapsody about Franco and his colleagues, who are treated as nothing less than angels. . . . he repeats every exploded

> propagandist rationalization of the Cause to which he adheres, every inversion of the witnessed fact (such as that the 'Reds' destroyed Guernica). . . .

Campbell's retort, written from Toledo and published four weeks later, is in strident terms that resemble his poetic manner:

> . . . the shameless, whining, and hypocritical tartufferies of Mr Spender about 'brutality', 'justice' and 'freedom' have a very queer smell and a very plaintive sound. For him to talk about truth when the sawdust is visibly running out of him in the shape of appeals to a bourgeois morality which he has always pretended to deride is an abject confession of the final abortion in defeat of all he pretended to stand for.

As this confrontation suggests, the Spanish Civil War brought into the open issues much larger than those related specifically to Spain and its internal agonies.

The heavy loss of life during the Civil War involved civilians as well as those engaged in fighting, and Guernica, a Basque village destroyed in a surprise attack by German bombers on a busy market day, became a byword for the wanton infliction of death and suffering upon the defenceless. (The painting based on this incident by the Spanish artist Pablo Picasso is one of the most famous works of art of the twentieth century and has what has been called the greatest theme of the artist's life.) G.L. Steer, who was an eye witness of the events in Guernica on 26 April 1937, described them in an essay published in August of that year:

> Monday was the weekly market day of Gernika, when the town existed. At about four-thirty the market, in summer, was at its fullest. The civil war had not made great difference to the Gernika farmers who brought in their animals and produce for sale from the rich valley. Rather there was better business. In Gernika, where the population was usually seven thousand, there were now an additional three thousand

refugees and two Basque battalions, who had plenty of pesetas to spend. . . .

After four there were farm carts coming into Gernika, rolling on solid wooden wheels and drawn by oxen whose heads were shaded under fleeces of sheep. Basque peasants in their long puckered market smocks walked backwards in front of them, mesmerizing the oxen to Gernika with their slim wands, with which they kept touching the horns and yoke gently. They talked to the oxen. Others were driving sheep to market. There was an assembly of animals near the parish church, a stately structure cavernous and dark within, standing upon a flight of thin steps like leaves piled one upon the other.

It is improbable that anyone was thinking about the war, when at four-thirty the church bell rang out loud. All over Spain a peal on a single bell is an air-raid warning. The population took cover, and the sheep in the square were left to their own devices.

There were numerous air-raid shelters in Gernika, constructed after the terrible raid on Durango on March 31st. Any cellar was covered with sandbags, and the entrance protected in the same way: a cardboard at the door painted ornamentally REFUGIO showed where the people had to dive. Though there had been few raid warnings at Gernika since the war began, the whole Basque population by now took their church bells seriously.

In a few minutes a Heinkel 111 came over and dropped six medium bombs, probably fifty-pounders, near the station, with a shower of grenades. A director of the railway company who was in the office rang up Bilbao to inform them that an aeroplane was bombing Gernika.

A few minutes later another Heinkel 111 appeared, to bomb the same area, but nearer the centre. The telephone with Bilbao was now cut. The plane from its slant and speedy sides machine-gunned the town at random, then veered homeward. . . .

Fifteen minutes passed, and the people were coming

> out of their shelters. A heavy drumming of engines was heard to the east. It was what we called in lighter moments the tranvias – the trams – the Junker 52's, who were so clumsy that they seemed to clang rather than to fly. These were the heaviest bombers that Germany had sent to Spain.

The rest of Steer's account emphasises the massiveness of the attack on this small community, and the completeness of the devastation:

> Over the town, whose streets were once more empty trenches, they dispersed their load a ton at a time. They turned woodenly over Gernika, the bombs fell mechanically in line as they turned. Then came the crack of the explosions; smoke stood up over Gernika like wool on a negro's head. Everywhere it sprouted, as more heavy bombers came.
>
> Besides many fifty- and hundred-pound bombs, they dropped great torpedoes weighing a thousand. Gernika is a compact little town, and most of these hit buildings, tearing them to pieces vertically from top to bottom and below the bottom. They penetrated refuges. The spirit of the people had been good, but now they panicked.
>
> An escort of Heinkel 51's, the same perhaps that had molested us that afternoon, were waiting for this moment. Till now they had been machine-gunning the roads round Gernika, scattering, killing or wounding sheep and shepherds. As the terrified population streamed out of the town they dived low to drill them with their guns. Women were killed here whose bodies I afterwards saw. It was the same technique as that used at Durango on March 31st, nearly a month back. . . . The terrified people lay face down in ditches, pressed their backs against tree trunks, coiled themselves in holes, shut their eyes and ran across sweet green open meadow. Many were foolish, and fled back before the aerial tide into the village. It was then that the heavy bombing of Gernika began.

It was then that Gernika was smudged out of that rich landscape, the province of Vizcaya, with a heavy fist.

It was about five-fifteen. For two hours and a half flights of between three and twelve aeroplanes, types Heinkel 111 and Junker 52, bombed Gernika without mercy and with system. They chose their sectors in the town in orderly fashion, with the opening points east of the Casa de Juntas and north of the Arms Factory. Early bombs fell like a circle of stars round the hospital on the road to Bermeo: all the windows were blown in by the divine efflatus, the wounded militiamen were thrown out of their beds, the inner fabric of the building shook and broke.

On the shattered houses, whose carpets and curtains, splintered beams and floors and furniture were knocked into angles and ready for the burning, the planes threw silver flakes. Tubes of two pounds, long as your forearm, glistening silver from their aluminium and elektron casing: inside them, as in the beginning of the world in Prometheus' reed, slept fire. Fire in a silver powder, sixty-five grammes in weight, ready to slip through six holes at the base of the glittering tube. So as the houses were broken to pieces over the people sheathed fire descended from heaven to burn them up.

The London Mercury, August 1937; repr. in *Spanish Front: Writers on the Civil War*, ed. Valentine Cunningham (1986).

It has often been pointed out that the attack on Guernica was like a ghastly dress-rehearsal for the bombing of civilian targets in the Second World War, and indeed German bombing techniques profited from their Spanish experience.

The special correspondent of *The Times*, James Holburn, arrived in Guernica a few hours after the raid had ended, and found it

a horrible sight, flaming from end to end. The reflection of the flames could be seen in the clouds of smoke above the mountains from 10 miles away. Throughout

> the night houses were falling until the streets became long heaps of red impenetrable debris.

His report, which appeared in *The Times* on 27 April, graphically recounts what happened:

> The whole town of 7,000 inhabitants, plus 3,000 refugees, was slowly and systematically pounded to pieces. Over a radius of five miles round a detail of the raiders' technique was to bomb separate *caserios*, or farmhouses. In the night these burned like little candles in the hills. All the villages around were bombed . . . and at Mugica, a little group of houses at the head of the Guernica inlet, the population was machine-gunned for 15 minutes. . .
>
> In the hospital of Josefinas, which was one of the first places bombed, all the 42 wounded militiamen it sheltered were killed outright. In a street leading downhill from the Casa de Juntas I saw a place where 50 people, nearly all women and children, are said to have been trapped in an air raid refuge under a mass of burning wreckage . . . an elderly priest named Aronategui was killed by a bomb while rescuing children from a burning house . . . it was utterly impossible even for firemen to enter the centre of the town. The hospitals . . . were glowing heaps of embers, all the churches except that of Santa Maria were destroyed and the few houses which still stood were doomed . . .

He also made clear the full significance of the event:

> In the form of its execution and the scale of the destruction it wrought, no less than in the selection of its objective, the raid . . . is unparalleled in military history. Guernica was not a military objective. A factory producing war material lay outside the town and was untouched. So were two barracks some distance from the town. . . . The object of the bombardment was seemingly the demoralization of the civil

> population and the destruction of the cradle of the Basque race.

War is not always as dramatic, or as horrific, as this, and in *Homage to Catalonia* Orwell captures the tedium and squalor of the military life as well as its excitement and sense of purpose:

> I wish I could convey to you the atmosphere of that time. . . . It is all bound up in my mind with the winter cold, the ragged uniforms of militiamen, the oval Spanish faces, the morse-like tapping of machine-guns, the smells of urine and rotting bread, the tinny taste of bean-stews, wolfed hurriedly out of unclean pannikins.
>
> The whole period stays by me with curious vividness. In my memory I live over incidents that might seem too petty to be worth recalling. . . .
>
> I am lying hidden among small fir-trees on the low ground west of Monte Oscuro, with Kopp and Bob Edwards and three Spaniards. Up the naked grey hill to the right of us a string of Fascists are climbing like ants. Close in front a bugle-call rings out from the Fascist lines. Kopp catches my eye and, with a schoolboy gesture, thumbs his nose at the sound.
>
> I am in the mucky yard at La Granja, among the mob of men who are struggling with their tin pannikins round the cauldron of stew. The fat and harassed cook is warding them off with the ladle. At a table nearby a bearded man with a huge automatic pistol strapped to his belt is hewing loaves of bread into five pieces. Behind me a Cockney voice (Bill Chambers, with whom I quarrelled bitterly and who was afterwards killed outside Huesca) is singing:
>
> There are rats, rats,
> Rats as big as cats,
> In the . . .
>
> A shell comes screaming over. Children of fifteen fling themselves on their faces. The cook dodges behind the

> cauldron. Everyone rises with a sheepish expression as the shell plunges and booms a hundred yards away.
>
> I am walking up and down the line of sentries, under the dark boughs of the poplars. In the flooded ditch outside the rats are paddling about, making as much noise as otters. As the yellow dawn comes up behind us, the Andalusian sentry, muffled in his cloak, begins singing. Across no man's land, a hundred or two hundred yards away, you can hear the Fascist sentry also singing.
>
> *Homage to Calalonia* (Penguin edn, 1966), pp.103–4.

Later, Orwell looked back at the war in relation to what it had achieved or failed to achieve, and to subsequent events in Europe (the following passage was originally published in 1943):

> I never think of the Spanish war without two memories coming into my mind. One is of the hospital ward at Lerida and the rather sad voices of the wounded militiamen singing some song with a refrain that ended –
>
> *Una resolucion,*
> *Luchar hast' al fin!*
> [A resolution, to continue the struggle to the end]
>
> Well, they fought to the end all right. For the last eighteen months of the war the Republican armies must have been fighting almost without cigarettes, and with precious little food. Even when I left Spain in the middle of 1937, meat and bread were scarce, tobacco a rarity, coffee and sugar almost unobtainable.
>
> The other memory is of the Italian militiaman who shook my hand in the guardroom, the day I joined the militia. I wrote about this man at the beginning of my book on the Spanish war [i.e., *Homage to Catalonia*], and do not want to repeat what I said there. When I remember – oh, how vividly! – his shabby uniform and fierce, pathetic, innocent face, the

> complex side-issues of the war seem to fade away and I see clearly that there was at any rate no doubt as to who was in the right. In spite of power politics and journalistic lying, the central issue of the war was the attempt of people like this to win the decent life which they knew to be their birthright. It is difficult to think of this particular man's probable end without several kinds of bitterness. Since I met him in the Lenin Barracks he was probably a Trotskyist or an Anarchist, and in the peculiar conditions of our time, when people of that sort are not killed by the Gestapo they are usually killed by the GPU. But that does not affect the long-term issues. This man's face, which I saw only for a minute or two, remains with me as a sort of visual reminder of what the war was really about. He symbolizes for me the flower of the European working class, harried by the police of all countries, the people who fill the mass graves of the Spanish battlefields and are now, to the tune of several millions, rotting in forced-labour camps.
>
> 'Looking Back on the Spanish War', *England Your England* (1953), pp.172–3.

In *The Thirties: A Dream Revolved* (1975) Julian Symons writes that

> The year 1936 was not only the middle of a decade, but also the heart of the Thirties dream. Consider: in this year the Left Book Club was founded, the Spanish Civil War began, the Surrealist Exhibition was held, the Jarrow Crusade took place, the first issue of *New Writing* appeared.
>
> Op. cit., p.55.

He adds that the 'political dream' included the hope and belief that 'Fascism would be checked abroad and at home', but the Spanish Civil War showed that the dream was groundless, and the triumph of Fascism led to the 'several millions, rotting in forced-labour camps' referred to by Orwell a few years later. Orwell himself in *Homage to Catalonia* had described his return to England, where the comfortably-off were

> sleeping the deep, deep sleep of England, from which I sometimes fear that we shall never wake till we are jerked out of it by the roar of bombs.

But the year of Orwell's book, 1938, was also the year of the Munich crisis, the 'roar of bombs' was not far off, and even the most complacent resident of southern England would be unable to ignore what was to happen in the closing years of the decade. The next chapter will be concerned with the events leading up to the outbreak of war on 3 September 1939.

4 The Road to the Second World War

A.J.P. Taylor has described the early work of Christopher Isherwood (1904–86) as 'uniquely representative of the thirties'. Isherwood belonged to the generation whose childhood saw the First World War (his father was killed in action). He was at school with W.H. Auden; later they became close friends, travelled to China together, and, just before the beginning of the Second World War, went to America together. Earlier, from 1929 to 1933, Isherwood lived in Germany, working as a teacher of English. His novels *Mr Norris Changes Trains* (1935; titled in the US *The Last of Mr Norris*) and *Goodbye to Berlin* (1939) are the only completed portions of what was intended to be (as Isherwood later said) 'a huge episodic novel of pre-Hitler Berlin' titled *The Lost*. Both are set in the period 1930–33 and present a portrait – part autobiographical, part documentary, part fictional – of Berlin in the years just before Hitler seized power.

Although unsuccessful in the presidential elections of 1932, Adolf Hitler (1899–1945) became Chancellor of Germany at the beginning of the following year, and before the year was out had in effect made himself dictator. The Nazi party crushed all opposition by ruthless means, and the burning of the Reichstag, the Berlin parliament building, in February 1933 by the Nazis (though blamed on the Communists) was a symbol of the destruction of parliamentary democracy in Hitler's Germany. Before long Germany was re-arming, in defiance of the Versailles Treaty, and had formed an 'axis' or alliance with Italy under its Fascist dictator Mussolini. There followed rapid military action: the invasion of Austria, the occupation of the Sudeten (German-speaking Czechoslovakia), and ultimately, after the Munich Agreement in September 1938 and a further year of uneasy peace, the invasion of Poland that precipitated the outbreak of war on 3 September 1939.

As Samuel Hynes has said, *Mr Norris Changes Trains* is concerned with the invasion of private lives by public events. The narrator, William Bradshaw (the author's own middle names), is an Englishman living in Berlin who has no particular interest in politics:

> Bradshaw knows no public figures, and has no public existence, being only a poor foreigner; but that private world is gradually invaded by the public world. . . . As public violence increases, the private life recedes, and the private man is drawn out of his closed world, into the streets. . . . [By the end of the novel] the public drama of Germany has been acted out to a tragic conclusion: in Berlin there is no private life left to be lived.
>
> *The Auden Generation*, pp. 178–81.

The following passage from the novel exemplifies this absorption of individuals into the swirling stream of contemporary history:

> Berlin was in a state of civil war. Hate exploded suddenly, without warning, out of nowhere; at street corners, in restaurants, cinemas, dance halls, swimming-baths; at midnight, after breakfast, in the middle of the afternoon. Knives were whipped out, blows were dealt with spiked rings, beer-mugs, chair-legs or leaded clubs; bullets slashed the advertisements on the poster-columns, rebounded from the iron roofs of latrines. In the middle of a crowded street a young man would be attacked, stripped, thrashed and left bleeding on the pavement; in fifteen seconds it was all over and the assailants had disappeared. Otto got a gash over the eye with a razor in a battle on a fairground near the Cöpernickerstrasse. The doctor put in three stitches and he was in hospital for a week. The newspapers were full of death-bed photographs

> of rival martyrs, Nazi, Reichsbanner and Communist. My pupils looked at them and shook their heads, apologizing to me for the state of Germany. "Dear, dear!" they said, "it's terrible. It can't go on."
>
> *Mr Norris Changes Trains* (1935), pp. 130–1.

In such an atmosphere, even the German language is contaminated:

> The murder reporters and the jazz-writers had inflated the German language beyond recall. The vocabulary of newspaper invective (traitor, Versailles-lackey, murder-swine, Marx-crook, Hitler-swamp, Red-pest) had come to resemble, through excessive use, the formal phraseology of politeness employed by the Chinese. The word *Liebe*, soaring from the Goethe standard, was no longer worth a whore's kiss. *Spring, moonlight, youth, roses, girl, darling, heart, May*: such was the miserably devaluated currency dealt in by the authors of all those tangoes, waltzes and fox-trots which advocated the private escape. Find a dear little sweetheart, they advised, and forget the slump, ignore the unemployed. Fly, they urged us, to Hawaii, to Naples, to the Never-Never-Vienna.
>
> Ibid., p.132.

The Nazis come to power in a Germany crushed first by defeat and the humiliating peace settlement, then by the recession. Widespread unemployment generates political apathy:

> And morning after morning, all over the immense, damp, dreary town and the packing-case colonies of huts in the suburb allotments, young men were waking up to another workless empty day to be spent as they could best contrive; selling bootlaces, begging, playing draughts in the hall of the Labour Exchange, hanging about urinals, opening the doors of cars, helping with crates in the markets, gossiping, lounging, stealing,

> overhearing racing tips, sharing stumps of cigarette-ends picked up in the gutter, singing folk-songs for groschen in courtyards and between stations in the carriages of the Underground Railway. After the New Year, the snow fell, but did not lie; there was no money to be earned by sweeping it away. The shop-keepers rang all coins on the counter for fear of the forgers.
>
> Ibid., p.133.

For a parallel and roughly contemporary account of the unemployed in Vienna, we can turn to John Lehmann's autobiography:

> [A young Austrian friend who was unemployed] had grown moody, bitter. . . . He had made several attempts at suicide and had long gashes on one of his wrists; he would often involve himself in brawls with the police solely in order to get into prison and have a few days' prison food. There were thousands like Heini in Vienna. As the iron winter of Central Europe closed down, the desperate, rotting horror of their existence, without adequate food or heating or clothes, seemed to me to reach its climax; as I watched the first snow falling on the roofs and domes of the city from the windows of my new eyrie, only prison thoughts came to me, a clenching of the fists to live through this evil time, for all those I knew and loved in Vienna to survive to better days; and yet, paradoxically, the arrival of the snow was a moment of relief and opportunity, for the Municipality had sudden need of an army of auxiliary street-sweepers, into which Heini and his unemployed friends were all likely to be enrolled for a few days.
>
> *The Whispering Gallery* (1955), pp.223–4.

Isherwood's Mr Norris, a seedy confidence-trickster, has been seen by Brian Finney as a personification of 'the tissue of lies, evasions and deceit which also characterises the sexual and political underworlds of Berlin in the novel' (*Christopher Isherwood: A Critical Biography*, 1979, p.112). The wig and cosmetics with which Norris conceals his baldness and bad complexion are private symbols of public deception. Finney adds:

> [Norris's] self-centred hedonism in fact parallels the attitudes of the Berlin population at large during the final years of the Weimar Republic. His sexual masochism is like their political self-abasement. His distortion of language to conceal the truth from Bradshaw and everyone else is paralleled by the debasement of linguistic meaning by the politicians and the press as the political confrontation between the right and the left heightens. And like them he is made to pay for his abandonment of responsibility by the escalating intrusion of public affairs into his private life.
>
> Op. cit., pp.115–16.

Norris is even 'a comic inversion of the far more skilful and successful machinations by which Hitler is simultaneously usurping political power', and it is Hitler's shadow that 'darkens the closing pages of the novel' (pp.116–17). Towards the end of the novel the narrative has reached March 1933, and evidence of Nazi power and Nazi policies is to be seen in the streets of Berlin:

> Early in March, after the elections, it turned suddenly mild and warm. "Hitler's weather," said the porter's wife; and her son remarked jokingly that we ought to be grateful to van der Lubbe, because the burning of the Reichstag had melted the snow. "Such a nice-looking boy," observed Frl. Schroder, with a sigh. "However could he go and do a dreadful thing like that?" The porter's wife snorted.
>
> Our street looked quite gay when you turned into it and saw the black-white-red flags hanging motionless from windows against the blue spring sky. On the

Nollendorfplatz people were sitting out of doors before the café in their overcoats, reading about the *coup d'état* in Bavaria. Göring spoke from the radio horn at the corner. Germany is awake, he said. An ice-cream shop was open. Uniformed Nazis strode hither and thither, with serious, set faces, as though on weighty errands. The newspaper readers by the café turned their heads to watch them pass and smiled and seemed pleased.

They smiled approvingly at these youngsters in their big, swaggering boots who were going to upset the Treaty of Versailles. They were pleased because it would soon be summer, because Hitler had promised to protect the small tradesmen, because their newspapers told them that the good times were coming. They were suddenly proud of being blonde. And they thrilled with a furtive, sensual pleasure, like schoolboys, because the Jews, their business rivals, and the Marxists, a vaguely defined minority of people who didn't concern them, had been satisfactorily found guilty of the defeat and the inflation, and were going to catch it.

The town was full of whispers. They told of illegal midnight arrests, of prisoners tortured in the S.A. barracks, made to spit on Lenin's picture, swallow castor-oil, eat old socks. They were drowned by the loud, angry voice of the Government, contradicting through its thousand mouths.

Mr Norris Changes Trains (1935), pp.263–4.

Isherwood's later novel covers the same period of history. Beginning in the autumn of 1930 and ending in the winter of 1932–3, *Goodbye to Berlin* consists of what the author later called a 'short loosely-connected sequence of diaries and sketches'. As in the earlier novel, public events gradually force themselves upon private experience, and such developments as Nazi anti-Semitism loom larger in the latter part of the book. The following passage recounts an early manifestation of feeling against the Jews:

> One night in October 1930, about a month after the Elections, there was a big row on the Leipzigerstrasse. Gangs of Nazi roughs turned out to demonstrate against the Jews. They manhandled some dark-haired, large-nosed pedestrians, and smashed the windows of all the Jewish shops. The incident was not, in itself, very remarkable; there were no deaths, very little shooting, not more than a couple of dozen arrests. I remember it only because it was my first introduction to Berlin politics.
>
> Frl. Mayr [the narrator's landlady], of course, was delighted: "Serve them right!" she exclaimed. "This town is sick with Jews. Turn over any stone, and a couple of them will crawl out. They're poisoning the very water we drink! They're strangling us, they're robbing us, they're sucking our life-blood. Look at all the big department stores: Wertheim, K.D.W., Landauers'. Who owns them? Filthy thieving Jews!"
>
> "The Landauers are personal friends of mine," I retorted icily, and left the room before Frl. Mayr had time to think of a suitable reply.
>
> *Goodbye to Berlin* (Chatto and Windus, edn, 1952), p.219.

However, events in Germany and in Europe had moved very rapidly between the period referred to here and the publication of the novel in 1939, in the same month as Auden's elegy on W.B. Yeats (to be referred to later). As Hynes has said, when it appeared, 'it must have seemed almost an historical novel – a record of a time and a mood long past' (p.358). The interest of Isherwood's two novels is that they evoke, obliquely but vividly, the atmosphere of life in Berlin in the crucial years that saw Hitler's rise to power.

Some reactions to the phenomenon of Hitlerism are summarised by Malcolm Muggeridge:

> Perhaps Hitler's greatest asset, abroad as well as at home, was the incredulity which his intentions aroused. They were so confused, seemed so fantastic,

> that it was difficult to believe they were seriously entertained even by those who supported him. . . . Even when the Nazi vote increased enormously, still few envisaged the possibility of his becoming Chancellor; even when he had become Chancellor, it was confidently assumed that he was no more than a puppet figure, easily manipulated by forces behind the scenes. . . .
>
> As the wonder of Hitler's achievement of power became accustomed, he became an obsession. His voice was often heard, families gathering round radio sets to listen, fascinated and appalled, to this shrill frenzy, an alien sound to fill their quiet sitting-rooms. . . . Newspapers were full of his doings and his photographs; his book, *Mein Kampf*, was often quoted. . . . His features, his little moustache, his drooping hair, became most familiar. Stock exchanges fluctuated with his moods. . . . It is doubtful if any human being in his lifetime has ever before so focused the attention of his fellows, so stirred up in them hatred or admiration, or, more often, a mixture of both.
>
> *The Thirties* (1940; repr. 1967), pp.253–4, 256–7.

But even before Hitler gained power, German rearmament was a source of concern to some. Winston Churchill, mindful of German bitterness over the Versailles Treaty, told the House of Commons on 23 November 1932:

> All these bands of sturdy Teutonic youths, marching along the streets and roads of Germany, with the light in their eyes of desire to suffer for their Fatherland, are not looking for [national] status. They are looking for weapons, and, when they have the weapons, believe me they will then ask for the return, the restoration of lost territories and lost colonies.

By the middle of the decade, some in England were beginning to issue warnings of impending war. The famous journalist

J.L. Garvin wrote in *The Observer* on 2 June 1935 of 'the plain undoubted probability that Europe within the next two or three years will be brought to the brink of war', and his forecast was not far out. Later in the same year, a diplomat, Sir Robert Vansittart, wrote:

> The Germans are themselves giving us far clearer warning than we had before 1914; and we have the remedy – rearmament – in our hands if we are quick enough,

prefacing this comment with the warning that '*there is not a week to lose in our measures*'. The shadow of coming war and a sense of the urgent need to prepare for war lay heavily over the second half of the decade, but those who urged full-scale rearmament met with opposition from the Government of the day. On 5 November 1936 Churchill again spoke against the half-hearted measures that were being taken:

> When we speak of the reign of law we must mean a reign of law supported by adequate and, if possible, by overwhelming force. The days of saving money on armaments have gone by. They may well return in happier conditions, but in this grim year 1936, and still more in its ominous successor, our aim, our task is not to reduce armaments. It is something even more intense, even more vital, namely, to prevent war if war can be staved off.

Two and a half years later, and a few weeks after Hitler's annexation of Austria, Churchill was still finding it necessary to issue similar warnings to an unheeding Government led by Neville Chamberlain:

> We are now in the third year of openly avowed rearmament. Why is it, if all is going well, there are so many deficiencies? Why, for instance, are the

> Guards drilling with flags instead of machine guns and anti-tank rifles?
>
> This and other extracts are included in Martin Gilbert's *Britain and Germany between the Wars* (1964).

At this point war was little more than a year away.

There were also some outside Parliament and politics who drew public attention to the tyrannies of European dictators and the threat of war. W.R. Inge, for instance, who was one of the contributors to a symposium on *The Causes of War* (1935), warned that 'Another war would very likely be the end of Western civilization' (p.19). Inge (1860–1954), a distinguished churchman, was Dean of St Paul's until 1934 and a popular preacher and prolific writer who reached a wide public through his journalism. For a quarter of a century from 1921 he contributed a weekly article to the London *Evening Standard* in which he commented on a wide range of political, social and moral issues. His questioning of accepted notions of 'progress' and 'democracy' and his attacks on the optimism of those who believed that the Great War had rendered another war impossible earned him the nickname of 'the gloomy dean'. After half a century his journalism has lost most of its force, but there are passages in which it is still possible to have a sense of the original impact of his articles on the ordinary reader. In a piece titled 'Torture comes back' he writes:

> This sinister reversion to barbarism is very surprising to us, because horror of cruelty is the strongest moral sentiment that we have.
>
> How then can human nature have suddenly become so much worse, as it seems to have done in some foreign countries which we looked upon as our friendly rivals in civilization?
>
> I have no doubt that the Great War accustomed men to scenes of death and suffering, and introduced a harsher tone into human society. But it is unhappily also true that our humanity is only skin deep.

> If we saw such horrors as have been common in some countries in and since the war, our sensibilities would very soon be blunted. There is hardly any other part of human nature in which the most shocking depravity lies so little below the surface.
>
> But in political trials, which have occasioned the worst brutalities, we must remember that the terrorists are themselves in terror. . . . And they have schooled themselves to believe that what used to be called reasons of State justify any cruelty and any treachery. . . .
>
> *Our Present Discontents* (1938), p.240.

What can now be seen with hindsight as the blatant menace of Hitler and German rearmament did not, however, shake the confidence of the majority in Britain, who continued to believe, almost to the last moment, that war was unthinkable or at any rate could be avoided:

> 'The King', [George V] wrote to the Duke of Connaught on 14 March 1932, 'never had such a good set of Ministers & it is wonderful how we can put a strong team into the field whenever required. . . . Geneva, India, Round Table Conference, Lausanne, Ottawa, Paris – even our second eleven would defeat most other countries. At the present time I do not think the prestige of our country has ever stood so high.'
>
> Signor Mussolini and Herr Hitler did not envisage their own ambitions or requirements in cricketing terms. They were perfectly prepared to use the League of Nations, so long as it served their purposes; the moment it became inconvenient, they were resolved to defy its mandates, calculating that such defiance would not, owing to the pacific intentions of the European Powers, and the isolationism of the United States, expose them to any very serious danger. They proved, for a while, correct in this calculation.
>
> There were a few who, even in 1933, were alert to the coming danger. In the House of Commons, on 26 May, Sir Austen Chamberlain expressed the view that

internal developments in Germany might constitute 'a menace to the whole world'. On June 13 Mr [Clement] Attlee pleaded that some assistance should be accorded to Austria to enable her to resist an inevitable German aggression. Mr Robert Boothby had already, in a prophetic speech, warned the House of Commons that, in view of Germany's military revival, and her clandestine Luftwaffe, our air estimates were ridiculously inadequate. On February 7, 1934, and again on March 8, Mr Winston Churchill forecast that before long Herr Hitler would possess a powerful German Air Force, and added that he 'dreaded the day when the means of threatening the heart of the British Empire should pass into the hands of the present rulers of Germany'. 'The support that Mr Winston Churchill received,' the Prime Minister [Ramsay MacDonald] reported blandly to the King, 'came only from a very small group of Members'.

The first serious shock to public complacency occurred in the autumn of 1933, when Herr Hitler, not meeting with the deference that he desired, ordered his delegation to leave the Disarmament Conference and to shake the dust of Geneva from their feet. . . .

Throughout 1934, while Herr Hitler was consolidating his despotism, British and French Ministers continued to believe, and then to hope, that time was on their side. . . .

The introduction by Herr Hitler of compulsory military service, coupled with the failure of the Berlin conversations, caused disquiet in Great Britain. Mr Baldwin, in the House of Commons, agreed that 'a measure of re-equipment' must now be undertaken. Lord Cranborne, at that date Mr Eden's Parliamentary Private Secretary, shocked the House by stating that, if we assumed the leadership and took a clear and firm line, war might possibly be averted; but that if we continued to hesitate and 'shilly-shally', then nothing remained but 'disaster complete and irrecoverable'. Mr Winston Churchill in solemn words warned an uneasy Parliament that we were entering 'a corridor of deepening and darkening danger along which we should be forced to move, perhaps for months, perhaps for years'.

Harold Nicolson, *King George the Fifth: His Life and Reign* (1952), pp.520–3.

The second half of the decade saw a series of crises culminating in the outbreak of war in the closing months of the Thirties.

An international crisis was expected in 1935 when a plebiscite was to be held in the Saar district, where the French had been working the coalfields since 1919 as a means of exacting reparations. But the plebiscite passed off peacefully under the supervision of the League of Nations and of British, French, and Italian troops: the choice for the Saarlanders was between returning to Germany, remaining under a League mandate, or attaching themselves to France. Well coaxed and threatened by the Nazis, they voted overwhelmingly in favour of return to Germany. Already in 1934 the Germans had reintroduced conscription without drawing more than a mild protest from the other European powers. This and the Saar plebiscite were the first Nazi victories in international affairs. Europe took them quietly, for most politicians had long since abandoned the pretence of pinning Germany down to the letter of the Versailles Treaty. They were willing now to make 'gentlemen's agreements', conceding some of the German claims. But the Germans remembered that they had signed the Versailles Treaty under duress; the continuance of the British blockade for six months after the Armistice and the quartering of French colonial troops on their soil were memories that seemed to acquit them of all duty to act as 'gentlemen' in the Franco-British sense.

A crisis did arise in 1935: not from German but from Italian action. It began with Italian provocation of the Abyssinians on the undelimited frontier between Abyssinia and Italian Somaliland; both Governments

> lodged protests at Geneva. The League set up its usual Commission to examine the problem. It seemed at first as though the Italians might not make war, if given a few concessions. When Pierre Laval, the French Prime Minister, had cordial talks with Mussolini in January 1935 the British Left Press interpreted them as a sinister move to dismember Abyssinia. . . .
>
> Robert Graves and Alan Hodge, *The Long Week-End: A Social History of Great Britain 1918–1939* (1940), pp.323–4.

Although many people in Britain sympathised with the Abyssinian cause, there was a reluctance to re-arm and to become involved in war. Most preferred to pin their faith on the League of Nations and economic sanctions, but neither was effective in dealing with Mussolini:

> By September, Italian troops were sailing for East Africa, the Italian delegation had walked out of the League, and the Committee of Five, which was dealing with the Abyssinian dispute, had reached a deadlock. Early in October Mussolini declared that Italy had been 'provoked', and that 'the time had come'. On October 3rd Italian troops went into action and on October 6th they captured the town of Adowa. Since the Italians had not taken revenge for the humiliating defeat inflicted on them by the Abyssinians at Adowa in the Nineties, it was felt that a compromise might be reached. A plan drawn up by Sir Samuel Hoare, the Foreign Secretary, and Pierre Laval, for France, offered Italy territorial and economic concessions which would have virtually turned Abyssinia into an Italian protectorate. But before the plan had been officially approved by any government, news of it reached the Press and raised an outburst of indignation in both Britain and France: the Abyssinians were being let down, aggression was being condoned, League principles wilfully betrayed. Sir Samuel Hoare, made scapegoat, was compelled to resign.
>
> Ibid., p.325.

The upshot was the defeat of the Abyssinian army and 'the *de facto* Italian conquest of Abyssinia': armed aggression and the ambitions of a dictator had been allowed to succeed.

It was clear by now that any future war would be different from the wars of the past in its use of aeroplanes:

> The Abyssinian crisis was the first to awaken people to the dangers of air-attack, though politicians had for some time been issuing warnings on air-raids, and planning to increase the R.A.F. Baldwin had said in the House in November 1932: 'I think it is well for the man in the street to realize that there is no power on earth that can prevent him from being bombed. Whatever people may tell him, the bomber will always get through. . . . The only defence is in offence, which means that you have to kill women and children more quickly than the enemy if you want to save yourselves.'
>
> Ibid., p.326.

Bernard Bergonzi has noted that 'Images of bombing were increasingly common in the poetry of the later Thirties, particularly after aerial bombing became widespread during the Spanish Civil War' (*Reading the Thirties*, p.105). A poem by Auden written in January 1937 begins:

> It's farewell to the drawing-room's civilised cry.
> The professor's sensible whereto and why,
> The frock-coated diplomat's social aplomb,
> Now matters are settled with gas and with bomb
>
> 'Song for the New Year'

and the dedicatory sonnet of his sequence *In Time of War*, which belongs to the following year, speaks of a place 'where the bombs are real and dangerous'. Among other poets cited by Bergonzi as expressing 'horrified responses' to air attacks on civilian targets is C. Day Lewis, whose 'Bombers' begins:

Black as vermin, crawling in echelon
Beneath the cloud-floor, the bombers come:
The heavy angels, carrying harm in
Their wombs that ache to be rid of death

and a later poem by the same writer, 'Battle of Britain', describes

A tangle
Of vapour trails, a vertiginously high
Swarming of midges . . .

as battle rages in the air.

In his *British Writers of the Thirties* (pp.200–3) Valentine Cunningham has adduced many other examples to show that 'fears of aerial bombardment' were not only commonplace in the decade but recur repeatedly in its literature, even before 'The realization that England was as open to the sky as any bombed city in Europe or China inspired the panicky digging of air-raid trenches during the "phoney war" period of September 1938 and the distribution of 38 million gas masks'. In Henry Green's novel *Party Going* (1939) the sight of a crowd on a railway platform prompts the comment, 'What targets, what targets for a bomb'. In Stephens Spender's play *Trial of a Judge* (1938) the Fascists sing that 'Our language/Will be the bomber's drum on the sky's skin', and MacNeice's *Autumn Journal*, published in the same year, anticipates the bombers 'Droning over from Majorca/To maim or blind or kill'. As Cunningham tells us, 'Poems stirred by bombing-plane horrors simply poured out: William Plomer's "The Japanese Invasion of China", Jacob Bronowski's "Bomber", Spender's "The Bombed Happiness", Herbert Read's "Bombing Casualties", [Geoffrey] Grigson's "The Bombers", George Barker's "Elegy on Spain" '.

But the Italian conquest of Abyssinia was only the curtain-raiser to a series of acts of aggression by Hitler's Germany. Once the powerlessness of the League of Nations and the reluctance of the great European powers to become involved in war had been demonstrated, Hitler proceeded to send his troops into the demilitarised zone of the Rhineland and, as we have seen, invaded Austria and seized part of Czechoslovakia. Britain came very close to war in 1938 and conflict was postponed only by the policy of appeasement followed by the Prime Minister, Neville Chamberlain, whose meeting with Hitler in Munich led to Britain's acquiescence in the German aggression against Austria and made 'Munich' a by-word for weakness and foolish trust in the word of a dictator. The then Foreign Secretary, Anthony Eden, described the crisis in his memoirs:

> The Fleet was finally mobilized on September 27th and by the next day war seemed imminent. I was in my seat in the crowded House of Commons when Chamberlain described the course of events. A scrap of paper was passed along to him. He glanced at it and then announced that Hitler had invited Mussolini, Daladier [Prime Minister of France] and himself to Munich. Members of all parties rose to their feet, cheered and waved their order papers. I did not feel I could take part in this scene, neither did Churchill. . . .
>
> On paper, the Munich Agreement which resulted from this meeting of the four heads of Goverments was more plausible than the Godesberg terms. In practice, the Czechs suffered as badly under the one as they would have done under the other. Worst of all was Mr Chamberlain's conviction, perfectly sincere in my opinion, that he was in the way to bringing about world appeasement. The negotiations were concluded in the early hours of September 30th. Later that morning, taking Hitler to one side, Chamberlain had asked whether he would be willing to sign a declaration. The Chancellor, of course, assented, and the two men thereupon put their names to the following document:
>
>> We, the German Führer and Chancellor, and the British Prime Minister, have had a further meeting today, and are agreed in recognizing that the question of Anglo-German relations is of the first import-

> ance for the two countries and for Europe.
>
> We regard the agreement signed last night, and the Anglo-German Naval Agreement, as symbolic of the desire of our two peoples never to go to war with one another again.
>
> We are resolved that the method of consultation shall be the method adopted to deal with any other questions that may concern our two countries and we are determined to continue our efforts to remove possible sources of difference, and thus to contribute to assure the peace of Europe. . . .

The Prime Minister, on returning home, waved this piece of paper to the crowd at Heston airport and in Downing Street called the Munich Agreement 'peace with honour. I believe it is peace for our time.' Seven months later, the Anglo-German Naval Agreement was denounced by Hitler. Eleven months later we were at war.

Earl of Avon, *The Eden Memoirs: The Reckoning* (1965), pp.28–9.

Another politician of the day, who, like Eden, was later to become Prime Minister, wrote of the 'peace with honour' agreement:

> This bit of paper [Chamberlain] had drawn up himself. He regarded it as of supreme importance. Hitler had signed it, without taking the trouble to do more than read it cursorily. It meant nothing.
>
> Chamberlain came back in triumph, to a concentration of applause and even adulation hardly ever granted to any statesman in our history. It was perhaps a demonstration of relief, but it was genuine and almost universal. . . . From every part of the globe, congratulations poured in.

Harold Macmillan, *Winds of Change 1914–1939* (1966), p.562.

The same writer describes the aftermath of Munich:

> So we embarked upon what has been called 'the golden age of appeasement'. The dream was to be rudely shattered six months later. On 15 March 1939 Hitler's proclamation to the German people contained this simple but dramatic sentence: 'Czechoslovakia has ceased to exist'.
>
> Ibid. p.568.

The summer of 1939 was tense and ominous. On 2 August Churchill stated in the House of Commons:

> The situation in Europe is graver than it was at this time last year. The German Government have already 2,000,000 men under arms actually incorporated in their Army. When the new class joins before the end of August more than 500,000 will be added to this number automatically. All along the Polish frontier from Danzig to Cracow there are heavy massings of troops, and every preparation is being made for a speedy advance. There are five German divisions in a high state of mobility around Breslau alone. . . .
>
> I have been told – I may be wrong, but I have not always been wrong – that many of the public buildings and of the schools in large parts of Czechoslovakia, Bohemia certainly, have been cleared and prepared for the accommodation of wounded. But that is not the only place. There is a definite movement of supplies and troops through Austria towards the east.

One of Churchill's biographers, Martin Gilbert, comments on this passage:

> The details he had given, Churchill went on, constituted 'terribly formidable signs'. Even the Government recognized this. The Fleet was largely mobilized, the anti-aircraft gunners were at their stations and there were similar 'great preparations' among Britain's allies.
>
> *Winston S. Churchill, Vol. V, 1922–39* (1976), p.1097.

Yet at this very moment Parliament was about to adjourn for the summer recess, and astonishingly Chamberlain refused to recall it in the last week of August, when war was only a few days away. In Churchill's words, there was at that time 'a hush all over Europe, nay, over all the world':

> Alas! it is the hush of suspense, and in many lands it is the hush of fear. Listen! No, listen carefully; I think I hear something – yes, there it was quite clear. Don't you hear it? It is the tramp of armies crunching the gravel of the parade-grounds, splashing through rain-soaked fields, the tramp of two million German soldiers and more than a million Italians – 'going on manoeuvres' – yes, only on manoeuvres!
>
> Of course it's only manoeuvres – just like last year. After all, the Dictators must train their soldiers. They could scarcely do less in common prudence, when the Danes, the Dutch, the Swiss, the Albanians – and of course the Jews – may leap out upon them at any moment and rob them of their living-space, and make them sign another paper to say who began it.
>
> Broadcast to the USA on 8 August 1939, quoted by Gilbert, p.1099.

Churchill's heavy irony is at the expense of the appeasers, who still believed, against all the evidence, that war could be avoided. When it did break out on 3 September, Chamberlain was shattered. He said in Parliament that 'everything that I have worked for, everything that I have hoped for, everything that I have believed in during my public life, has crashed into ruins'; privately he wrote that 'the final long-drawn-out agonies that preceded the actual declaration of war were as nearly unendurable as could be.' (Keith Feiling, *The Life of Neville Chamberlain*, 1946, p.516.) In May of the following year, when the new decade was only a few months old, he relinquished the leadership to Churchill.

To a few at the time, and to many more afterwards, Chamberlain's phrase 'peace with honour' had a very hollow ring, since what had happened was nothing less than the betrayal of a small country in the interests of a short-lived and uneasy peace. For a whole generation 'Munich' became synonymous with moral cowardice and a final damning indictment of political policies and public morality in the Thirties. As Auden wrote, from New York, in his poem 'September 1, 1939':

> I sit in one of the dives
> On Fifty-Second Street
> Uncertain and afraid
> As the clever hopes expire
> Of a low dishonest decade:
> Waves of anger and fear
> Circulate over the bright
> And darkened lands of the earth,
> Obsessing our private lives;
> The unmentionable odour of death
> Offends the September night.
>
> *The English Auden*, p.245.

The 'waves of anger' were surely directed, at least partly, towards Chamberlain, as the national leader at the end of the 'low dishonest decade' that Auden saw expiring in a slide towards anarchy and barbarism.

In his poem 'Newsreel' C. Day Lewis issued a warning against the mass indifference to impending disaster that he detected around him: the cinema offers an escape from personal and public anxieties –

> Enter the dream-house, brothers and sisters, leaving
> Your debts asleep, your history at the door . . .

– and even the newsreels with their message of a world torn apart by violence ('the warplanes . . . Screaming hysteric treble') fail to convey the realization that this violence will soon

> Grow nearer home – and out of the dream-house stumbling
> One night into a strangling air and the flung

Rags of children and thunder of stone niagaras
tumbling,
You'll know you slept too long.

Looking back on the period after forty years, Stephen Spender recalled a similar sense of the familiar world menaced and threatened with extinction:

> Another still mysterious and unimaginable reality was the approaching war. Doubtless to the CND protesters of the fifties, the horrors of two world wars seemed nothing compared with those they anticipated with the falling of H-bombs. However, not knowing about atomic weapons, we anticipated the worst destruction then imaginable. In our minds, the Second World War would mean the end of civilization. By this we meant the total destruction of all major built-up areas. My own private fantasy was of emerging out of a cellar after the first air raid on London on to a scene which consisted entirely of ruins. Nor was this fantasy so far from what was anticipated by scientists. Gerald Heard, that erratic genius who used to broadcast on the BBC about the most recent scientific developments, told me of the effects of high explosives which would burn through steel girders as though they were straw. Just before the Munich agreement, Raymond Postgate showed me a map of London – with the docks, the sewage plants, the power stations all seeming defenceless and exposed – and described to me the appalling destruction which would result from the first great air raids on London.
>
> *The Thirties and After* (1978), pp.22–3.

Isherwood's *Prater Violet*, though not published until 1946, is set in 1933 and offers 'apocalyptic pictures of universal doom' in the words of Bergmann, a Viennese film director who has come to work in London:

> And then he would begin to describe the coming war. The attack on Vienna, Prague, London, Paris,

> without warning, by thousands of planes, dropping bombs filled with deadly bacilli; the conquest of Europe in a week; the subjugation of Asia, Africa, the Americas; the massacre of the Jews, the execution of intellectuals, the herding of non-Nordic women into enormous state brothels; the burning of paintings and books, the grinding of statues into powder; the mass-sterilization of the unfit, mass-murder of the elderly, mass-conditioning of the young; the reduction of France and the Balkan countries to wilderness, in order to make national parks for the Hitler Jugend; the establishment of Brown Art, Brown Literature, Brown Music, Brown Philosophy, Brown Science, and the Hitler Religion, with its Vatican at Munich and its Lourdes at Berchtesgaden; a cult based upon the most complex system of dogmas concerning the real nature of the Fuehrer, the utterances of *Mein Kampf*, the ten thousand Bolshevist heresies, and the sacrament of Blood and Soil; and upon elaborate rituals of mystic union with the Homeland, involving human sacrifice and the baptism of steel.
>
> *Prater Violet* (Penguin edn, 1961), pp.43–4.

Bergmann adds, referring to the diners in the restaurant where he is sitting, that ' "All these people . . . will be dead" '. Although Isherwood is obviously writing with the benefit of hindsight, and although not many of the predictions expressed by the speaker came to pass, he is in some measure conveying a sense of the deep anxiety that prevailed in the minds of some even at such an early date, when Hitler had only just come to power.

Orwell's novel *Coming Up For Air* was published on 12 June 1939. Its narrator, George Bowling, stout and middle-aged, recalls his childhood in pre-1914 England and sets out on a sentimental journey from the London suburb where he lives to the small town he grew up in. But nostalgia turns to sadness when he discovers that the community he knew no longer exists, having been swallowed by urban development. The pool where he once saw a giant carp and has always hoped some day to fish has been drained and is used as a rubbish-dump. Behind this personal disillusion – the sense of a world irrevocably changed for the worse – lurks the consciousness of impending war: when a bomber flies over, George reflects:

> In two years' time, one year's time, what shall we be doing when we see one of those things? Making a dive for the cellar, wetting our bags with fright.

And towards the end of the novel Orwell writes:

> War is coming, 1941, they say. And there'll be plenty of broken crockery, and little houses ripped open like packing-cases, and the guts of the chartered accountant's clerk plastered over the piano that he's buying on the never-never. . . . *It's all going to happen.* All the things you've got at the back of your mind, the things you're terrified of, the things that you tell yourself are just a nightmare or only happen in foreign countries. The bombs, the food-queues, the rubber truncheons, the barbed wire, the coloured shirts, the slogans, the enormous faces, the machine-guns squirting out of bedroom windows. It's all going to happen. . . .
>
> *Coming Up For Air* (Secker and Warburg edn, 1963), pp.227–8.

War came, of course, earlier than the passage predicted: within less than three months of the novel's publication Britain was at war with Germany, and the Battle of Britain, which saw innumerable 'little houses ripped open like packing-cases', followed in 1940.

The Irish poet W.B. Yeats, whose career had begun well before the end of the nineteenth century, died at the beginning of 1939; and in the memorial poem that W.H. Auden almost immediately composed his death is described in images of military action and crisis:

But for him it was his last afternoon as himself,
An afternoon of nurses and rumours;
The provinces of his body revolted,
The squares of his mind were empty,
Silence invaded the suburbs,
The current of his feeling failed. . . .

Later in the poem, after evoking Yeat's life and achievement, Auden turns to the present:

In the nightmare of the dark
All the dogs of Europe bark,
And the living nations wait,
Each sequestered in its hate;

Intellectual disgrace
Stares from every human face,
And the seas of pity lie
Locked and frozen in each eye.

'In Memory of W.B. Yeats', *The English Auden*, pp.241, 243.

In this, as in Auden's 'September 1, 1939', cited a little earlier in this chapter, there is a sense that it is not only the decade but civilisation itself that is dying. A similar note is sounded in one of the finest short lyrics of the period, MacNeice's 'The Sunlight on the Garden':

Our freedom as free lances
Advances towards its end;
The earth compels, upon it
Sonnets and birds descend;
And soon, my friend,
We shall have no time for dances. . . .

As Robin Skelton has said, 'Even before they were quite over, the thirties took on the appearance of myth; the poets themselves, looking back upon the events of those years, saw heroes and dragons in dramatic perspectives, and many of them uttered suitable valedictory sentiments'. (*Poetry of the Thirties*, 1964, p.13). One of the most explicit valedictions is 'Farewell Chorus' by a younger poet, David Gascoyne (born 1916):

And so let's take a last look-round, and say Farewell
 to all
Events that gave the last decade, which this New Year
Brings to its close, a special pathos. Let us fill
One final fiery glass and quickly drink to 'the Pre-
 War'
Before we greet 'the Forties,' whose unseen sphinx-
 face
Is staring fixedly upon us from behind its veil;
Drink farewell quickly, ere the Future smash the
 glass. . . .

To the delusive peace of those disintegrating years
Through which burst uncontrollably into our view
Successive and increasingly premonitory flares,
Explosions of the dangerous truth beneath, which no
Steel-plated self-deception could for long with-
 stand . . .
Years through the rising storm of which somehow we
 grew,
Struggling to keep an anchored heart and open mind,

Too often failing. Years through which none the less
The coaxing of complacency and sleep could still
 persuade
Kind-hearted Christians of the permanence of Peace,
Increase of common-sense and civic virtue. Years
 which bade
Less placid conscientious souls indignantly arise
Upon ten thousand platforms to proclaim the system
 mad

> And urge the liquidation of a senile ruling-class.
> Years like a prison-wall, frustrating though unsound,
> On which the brush of History, with quick, neurotic
> strokes,
> Its latest and most awe-inspiring fresco soon outlined:
> Spenglerian* lowering of the Western skies, red lakes
> Of civil bloodshed, free flags flagrantly torn down
> By order of macabre puppet orators, the blind
> Leading blindfolded followers into the Devil's den . . .

Gascoyne's poem is dated 'New Year 1940', so that it is, of course, a wartime poem. What is striking is the rapidity with which 'the Pre-War', barely four months distant, has receded into the past and 'the last decade' has assumed a recognisable shape.

A much older writer, E.M. Forster, reveals a persistent consciousness of the decade as a distinct phase of history in his 'Post-Munich', written in 1939 and collected in his *Two Cheers for Democracy* (1951). It begins:

> During the present decade thousands and thousands of innocent people have been killed, robbed, mutilated, insulted, imprisoned. We, the fortunate exceptions, learn of this from the newspapers and from refugees, we realize that it may be our turn next, and we know that all these private miseries may be the prelude to an incalculable catastrophe, in which the whole of western civilization and half oriental civilization may go down. Perhaps history will point to these years as the moment when man's inventiveness finally outbalanced his moral growth, and toppled him downhill.

Again, there is a sense of a recent past that is appalling to contemplate and a near future that is equally appalling to envisage. Forster's second paragraph refers to the decade as

*Oswald Spengler (1880–1936), German historian, offered in *The Decline of the West* (1918; English translation 1926) a cyclical view of history and foresaw the inevitable decline of western civilisation.

'tragic'; his final paragraph declares that 'This decade has lasted long enough'.

A 'tragic' decade, a 'low dishonest decade', a decade of 'Steel-plated self-deception': these were some of the instant verdicts on the Thirties, and they cannot be dismissed half a century later.

Postscript

In January 1940 food rationing was introduced in Britain. In April Germany invaded Norway and Denmark, and in the following month Holland, Belgium and Luxembourg. Chamberlain resigned as Prime Minister on 10 May and was succeeded by Churchill; on the 29th of the same month came the evacuation of Dunkirk, marking Britain's retreat from the continent of Europe. In June Italy entered the war and the Germans entered Paris; the Battle of Britain followed during the summer months.

Even the English language was suddenly invaded by new elements: terms such as 'blitz', 'blackout', 'evacuee' and 'air raid shelter' were on everyone's lips. Civilians found themselves in situations hitherto associated only with armed forces serving at a distance from home: fathers doing their stint of 'firewatching' or serving as 'air raid wardens' took their 'tin helmets' with them, and children had to be reminded to take their gas masks to school in case there was a poison gas attack during lesson-time. But all this is, of course, part of the history of another decade, the Forties.

Chronological Table

The following table, necessarily selective, lists under each year of the decade first some significant contemporary events and then some of the important publications that appeared.

Contemporary events	*Publications*
1930	
Ramsay MacDonald heads Labour Government elected in the previous year	W.H. Auden, *Poems*
Widespread unemployment in Britain and elsewhere	T.S. Eliot, *Ash Wednesday*
Nazi Party gains positions of power in Germany	William Empson, *Seven Types of Ambiguity*
France begins to construct the Maginot Line to defend its frontier with Germany	Sir James Jeans, *The Mysterious Universe*
Gandhi begins campaign of civil disobedience in India	J.M. Keynes, *Treatise on Money*
The planet Pluto is discovered	D.H. Lawrence, *A Propos of 'Lady Chatterley's Lover'*
Amy Johnson flies solo from London to Australia	Stephen Spender, *Twenty Poems*
Youth Hostels Association founded	Evelyn Waugh, *Vile Bodies*
Daily Worker, newspaper of the British Communist Party, begins publication	
Television broadcasting begins in the USA	
Death of D.H. Lawrence, Robert Bridges, Sir Arthur Conan Doyle	

1931

Economic crisis in Britain: (*August*) Ramsay MacDonald forms a National Government; (*September*) riots in London and Glasgow; Britain abandons the Gold Standard, and the pound falls dramatically on the international money market; 10 per cent cut in unemployment payments imposed as economy measure; introduction of Means Test; (*October*) General Election: MacDonald forms second National Government

Revolution in Spain

Statute of Westminster defines Dominion Status

Gandhi attends India Conference in London

Japan invades Manchuria

Death of Arnold Bennett

Roy Campbell, *The Georgiad*

C. Day Lewis, *From Feathers to Iron*

T.S. Eliot, *Thoughts after Lambeth*

James Hanley, *Boy*

Anthony Powell, *Afternoon Men*

Lytton Strachey, *Portraits in Miniature*

Virginia Woolf, *The Waves*

1932

Unemployment rises to 2.8 million in Britain (13.7m in USA, 5.6m in Germany)

Hunger marches organised in Britain

Policy of slum clearance initiated

Oswald Mosley forms British Union of Fascists

Geneva Disarmament Conference

Nazis continue to gain electoral successes in Germany

Fascist regime established in Portugal

F.D. Roosevelt becomes President of the USA

Scrutiny founded

Basic English founded

Death of Lytton Strachey, Lady Gregory

W.H. Auden, *The Orators*

T.S. Eliot, *Selected Essays; Sweeney Agonistes*

Aldous Huxley, *Brave New World*

Rudyard Kipling, *Limits and Renewals*

F.R. Leavis, *New Bearings in English Poetry*

Q.D. Leavis, *Fiction and the Reading Public*

Anthony Powell, *Venusberg*

Michael Roberts (editor), *New Signatures*

Evelyn Waugh, *Black Mischief*

1933

Hitler becomes German Chancellor	Ivy Compton-Burnett, *More Women than Men*
Burning of Reichstag, Berlin; Hitler assumes dictatorial powers; persecution of Jews begins in Germany; Trade unions are suppressed there; Germany leaves the League of Nations.	T.S. Eliot, *The Use of Poetry and the Use of Criticism*
Japan occupies North China and leaves the League of Nations	Walter Greenwood, *Love on the Dole*
New Deal inaugurated in USA	A.E. Housman, *The Name and Nature of Poetry*
Oxford Union passes motion indicating refusal to fight for King and Country	Malcolm Lowry, *Ultramarine*
	George Orwell, *Down and Out in Paris and London*
	Dorothy Sayers, *Murder Must Advertise*
	Stephen Spender, *Poems*
	W.B. Yeats, *Collected Poems*

1934

Fascist and anti-Fascist demonstrations in Hyde Park	T.S. Eliot, *After Strange Gods*
Depressed Areas Bill passed	E.M. Forster, *Goldsworthy Lowes Dickinson*
Peace Pledge Union formed in Britain	Robert Graves, *I, Claudius*
Expansion of the Royal Air Force	Graham Greene, *It's a Battlefield*
Churchill warns Parliament of German air menace	George Orwell, *Burmese Days*
Anglo-Russian trade agreement	Ezra Pound, *Make it New*
Queen Mary launched	Dorothy Sayers, *The Nine Tailors*
	Dylan Thomas, *Eighteen Poems*
	Evelyn Waugh, *A Handful of Dust*
	H.G. Wells, *Experiment in Autobiography*

1935

Silver Jubilee of King George V

(*June*) Stanley Baldwin forms National Government; (*November*) General Election at which National Government wins large majority

Anglo-German Naval Agreement

Saar restored to Germany

Germany rejects disarmament provisions of the Versailles Treaty and reintroduces compulsory military service

Italy invades Abyssinia; League of Nations imposes sanctions against Italy

London County Council Green Belt Scheme inaugurated

British Council formed

Left Book Club founded

Robert Watson-Watt builds radar equipment

French liner *Normandie* crosses the Atlantic in 107½ hours

Death of T.E. Lawrence ('Lawrence of Arabia')

W.H. Auden and Christopher Isherwood, *The Dog Beneath the Skin*

Cyril Connolly, *The Rock Pool*

C. Day Lewis, *A Time to Dance*

Walter de la Mare, *Poems 1919–34*

T.S. Eliot, *Murder in the Cathedral*

William Empson, *Poems*

Graham Greene, *England Made Me*

Patrick Hamilton, *Twenty Thousand Streets under the Sky*

Christopher Isherwood, *Mr Norris Changes Trains*

Louis MacNeice, *Poems*

L.H. Myers, *The Root and the Flower*

George Orwell, *A Clergyman's Daughter*

Sidney & Beatrice Webb, *Soviet Communism: A New Civilisation*

1936

(*January*) Death of George V; accession of Edward VIII; (*December*) Abdication of Edward VIII; accession of George VI

Jarrow March

Increase in British defence budget

Mosley leads anti-Jewish march in London

Germany occupies demilitarised zone of Rhineland

Mussolini announces Rome–Berlin axis

W.H. Auden, *Look, Stranger!*

W.H. Auden and Christopher Isherwood, *The Ascent of F6*

G.K. Chesterton, *Autobiography*

T.S. Eliot, *Collected Poems 1909–35*

E.M. Forster, *Abinger Harvest*

A.E. Housman, *More Poems*

Aldous Huxley, *Eyeless in Gaza*

James Joyce, *Collected Poems*

Italy annexes Abyssinia

Austria introduces conscription

(*July*) Spanish Civil War begins; (*November*) Siege of Madrid begins

Roosevelt re-elected President in USA

China declares war on Japan

Television service from Alexandra Palace, London, inaugurated by BBC

First holiday camp opened (at Skegness)

Olympic Games held in Berlin

New Writing begins publication

Penguin Books founded

Death of Rudyard Kipling, A.E. Housman, G.K. Chesterton

Rudyard Kipling, *Something of Myself*

D.H. Lawrence, *Phoenix*

T.E. Lawrence, *The Mint* (US publication)

George Orwell, *Keep the Aspidistra Flying*

Dylan Thomas, *Twenty-five Poems*

W.B. Yeats (editor), *Oxford Book of Modern Verse*

1937

(*May*) Retirement of Stanley Baldwin; Neville Chamberlain becomes Prime Minister; (*November*) Lord Halifax, Foreign Secretary, visits Hitler (starting the policy of appeasement)

Air Raid Precautions Bill passed

Matrimonial Causes Bill passed, making divorce easier in England and Wales

Destruction of Guernica (Spain)

Mussolini visits Berlin

Italy withdraws from League of Nations

Japanese capture Peking, Shanghai and Nanking

Jet engine invented

Death of J.M. Barrie, Ramsay MacDonald

W.H. Auden and Louis MacNeice, *Letters from Iceland*

Christopher Caudwell, *Illusion and Reality*

Aldous Huxley, *Ends and Means*

Christopher Isherwood, *Sally Bowles*

David Jones, *In Parenthesis*

Franz Kafka, *The Trial* (English translation)

George Orwell, *The Road to Wigan Pier*

J.B. Priestley, *Time and the Conways*

J.R.R. Tolkien, *The Hobbit*

Rex Warner, *The Wild Goose Chase*

Virginia Woolf, *The Years*

1938

(*March*) Germany invades and then annexes Austria

(*August*) Germany mobilises

(*September*) Chamberlain meets Hitler at Berchtesgaden; later he meets Hitler and Mussolini in Munich and agrees to the transfer of Sudetenland to Germany; The Royal Navy is mobilised

(*October*) Germany occupies the Sudetenland; Japan leaves the League of Nations; Italy annexes Libya

(*November*) Persecution of Jews increases in Germany and Italy

Franco gains victories in Spain

Japanese victories in China continue

The liner *Queen Elizabeth* is launched

The ball-point pen is invented

Picture Post begins publication

W.H. Auden (editor), *Oxford Book of Light Verse*

W.H. Auden and Christopher Isherwood, *On the Frontier*

Samuel Beckett, *Murphy*

Elizabeth Bowen, *The Death of the Heart*

Christopher Caudwell, *Studies in a Dying Culture*

Cyril Connolly, *Enemies of Promise*

Robert Graves, *Collected Poems 1914–38*

Graham Greene, *Brighton Rock*

Richard Hughes, *In Hazard*

Christopher Isherwood, *Lions and Shadows*

Louis MacNeice, *The Earth Compels*

George Orwell, *Homage to Catalonia*

Stevie Smith, *Over the Frontier*

Stephen Spender, *Trial of a Judge*

Rex Warner, *The Professor*

Evelyn Waugh, *Scoop*

W.B. Yeats, *Purgatory*

1939

(*January*) Chamberlain meets Mussolini in Rome; Franco captures Barcelona

(*February*) Britain recognises the Franco government in Spain and pledges to support Poland against aggression

(*March*) End of the Spanish Civil War

W.H. Auden and Christopher Isherwood, *Journey to a War*

Joyce Cary, *Mister Johnson*

T.S. Eliot, *The Family Reunion*; *The Idea of a Christian Society*

Robert Graves and Alan Hodge, *The Long Weekend*

Henry Green, *Party Going*

A.E. Housman, *Collected Poems*

(*April*) Italy invades Albania; conscription introduced in Britain

(*August*) Chamberlain fails to negotiate with Hitler; evacuation of women and children from London begins

(*September*) Germany invades Poland; (3rd) Britain and France declare war on Germany; the USSR invades Poland; British Expeditionary Force sent to France

(*October*) Sinking of HMS *Royal Oak*; German mines cause heavy British shipping losses

(*November*) USSR invades Finland

Ministry of Supply and Ministry of Information formed

Discovery of nuclear fission

Invention of DDT

British Overseas Airways Corporation established

Regular transatlantic commercial flights begun by Pan-American Airways

Horizon and *Poetry London* are founded

Death of W.B. Yeats, Ford Madox Ford, Sigmund Freud

Aldous Huxley, *After Many a Summer*

Christopher Isherwood, *Goodbye to Berlin*

James Joyce, *Finnegans Wake*

Louis MacNeice, *Autumn Journal*

George Orwell, *Coming up for Air*

Anthony Powell, *What's Become of Waring?*

H.G. Wells, *The Fate of Homo Sapiens*

A Guide to Reading

What follows represents a very small selection from the large amount of material available. Fuller information will be found in *The New Cambridge Bibliography of English Literature, Volume 4, 1900–1950*, edited by I.R. Willison (Cambridge University Press, 1972), which provides listings of both primary and secondary works for virtually all the writers referred to in this volume. The books by C.L. Mowat and A.J.P. Taylor contain valuable bibliographies of secondary works dealing with the political, social and economic history of the period. Valentine Cunningham's *British Writers of the Thirties* contains a comprehensive 'Working Bibliography'.

Primary Sources

Verse and Drama

W.H. Auden, *Poems* (1930); *The Orators* (1932); *Look, Stranger!* (1936); *Another Time* (1940). Auden's prose and verse of the period are usefully collected in *The English Auden: Poems, Essays and Dramatic Writings 1927–1939*, ed. Edward Mendelson (1977).

W.H. Auden and Christopher Isherwood, *The Dog Beneath the Skin* (1935); *The Ascent of F6* (1936); *On the Frontier* (1938); *Journey to a War* (1939).

W.H. Auden and Louis MacNeice, *Letters from Iceland* (1937).

John Betjeman, *Continual Dew: A little Book of Bourgeois Verse* (1937); *Collected Poems* (1958).

Roy Campbell, *The Georgiad* (1931); *Collected Poems* (3 vols, 1949–60).

C. Day Lewis, *From Feathers to Iron* (1931); *The Magnetic Mountain* (1933); *Collected Poems 1929–1933* (1935); *A Time to Dance* (1935); *Overtures to Death* (1938); *Poems in Wartime* (1940).

Louis MacNeice, *Poems* (1935); *The Earth Compels* (1938); *Autumn Journal* (1939); *Collected Poems* (1966).

Michael Roberts, *Poems* (1936); *Collected Poems* (1958).
Stephen Spender, *Poems* (1933); *Trial of a Judge* (1938); *Selected Poems* (1940); *Collected Poems 1928–1953* (1955).
Rex Warner, *Poems* (1937).

Anthologies

Valentine Cunningham (ed.), *The Penguin Book of Spanish Civil War Verse* (1980).
Ian MacDougall, *Voices from the Spanish War* (1986).
Michael Roberts (ed.), *New Signatures* (1932); *New Country* (1933); *The Faber Book of Modern Verse* (1936).
Robin Skelton, *Poetry of the Thirties* (1964).

Fiction

Walter Brierley, *Means Test Man* (1935).
A.J. Cronin, *The Stars Look Down* (1936)
Lewis Grassic Gibbon, *Sunset Song* (1932); *Cloud Howe* (1933); *Grey Granite* (1934). These three novels were reissued as a trilogy, *A Scots Quair* (1946).
Henry Green, *Party Going* (1939).
Graham Greene, *It's a Battlefield* (1934); *England Made Me* (1935); *Brighton Rock* (1938); *The Confidential Agent* (1939).
Walter Greenwood, *Love on the Dole* (1933).
Patrick Hamilton, *Twenty Thousand Streets under the Sky* (1935).
Geoffrey Household, *Rogue Male* (1939).
Aldous Huxley, *Brave New World* (1932).
Christopher Isherwood, *The Memorial* (1932); *Mr Norris Changes Trains* (1935); *Goodbye to Berlin* (1939).
Lewis Jones, *Cwmardy* (1937).
Arthur Koestler, *Spanish Testament* (1937); *Darkness at Noon* (1940).
George Orwell, *Burmese Days* (1934); *A Clergyman's Daughter* (1935); *Keep the Aspidistra Flying* (1936); *Coming up for Air* (1939).
Anthony Powell, *Afternoon Men* (1931); *Venusberg* (1932); *From a View to a Death* (1933); *Agents and Patients* (1936); *What's Become of Waring* (1939).
Rex Warner, *The Wild Goose Chase* (1937); *The Professor* (1938).
Evelyn Waugh, *Vile Bodies* (1930); *Black Mischief* (1932); *A Handful of Dust* (1934); *Scoop* (1938); *Work Suspended and Other Stories Written before the Second World War* (1948).

Autobiography and Miscellaneous Prose

Cyril Connolly, *Enemies of Promise* (1938); *The Condemned Playground: Essays 1927–1944* (1945).
John Cornford, *Collected Writings* (1986). Includes poems as well as essays and letters.
Valentine Cunningham, *Spanish Front: Writers on the Civil War* (1986).
C. Day Lewis, *The Buried Day* (1960).
T.S. Eliot, *After Strange Gods* (1934); *The Idea of a Christian Society* (1939).
E.M. Forster, *Two Cheers for Democracy* (1951); *Selected Letters of E.M. Forster, Volume II, 1921–1970*, ed. Mary Lago and P.N. Furbank (1985).
Christopher Isherwood, *Lions and Shadows* (1938).
F.R. Leavis and Denys Thompson, *Culture and Environment* (1933).
John Lehmann, *The Whispering Gallery* (1955).
F.L. Lucas, *Journal under the Terror, 1938* (1938).
George Orwell, *Down and Out in Paris and London* (1933); *The Road to Wigan Pier* (1937); *Homage to Catalonia* (1938); *Inside the Whale* (1940); *Collected Essays, Journalism and Letters of George Orwell*, ed. Sonia Orwell and Ian Angus, 4 vols. (1968).
J.B. Priestley, *English Journey* (1934).
Bertrand Russell, *The Autobiography of Bertrand Russell, Vol. II, 1914–1944* (1968).
Stephen Spender, *World within World* (1951).
Evelyn Waugh, *Remote People* (1931), *Waugh in Abyssinia* (1936); *The Diaries of Evelyn Waugh*, ed. Michael Davie (1976); *The Letters of Evelyn Waugh*, ed. Mark Amory (1980).
Leonard Woolf, *Downhill All the Way* (1967).
Virginia Woolf, *The Letters of Virginia Woolf*, ed. Nigel Nicolson, Vols 4–6 (1978–80); *The Diary of Virginia Woolf*, ed. A.O. Bell, Vols 4–5 (1982–4).

Secondary Sources

Bernard Bergonzi, *Reading the Thirties* (1978).
Ronald Blythe, *The Age of Illusion* (1963).
Noreen Branson and Margot Heinemann, *Britain in the Nineteen Thirties* (1971).
Ronald Carter, *Thirties Poets: 'The Auden Group'* (1984).

J. Clark, M. Heinemann, D. Margolies and C. Smee (eds), *Culture and Crisis in Britain in the 30s* (1979).
G.D.H. and M.I. Cole, *The Condition of Britain* (1937).
Valentine Cunningham, *British Writers of the Thirties* (1988).
G.S. Fraser, *The Modern Writer and his World* (1964).
Martin Gilbert, *Britain and Germany between the Wars* (1964); *The Roots of Appeasement* (1966).
Robert Graves and Alan Hodge, *The Long Week-end: A Social History of Great Britain 1918–1939* (1940).
Samuel Hynes, *The Auden Generation: Literature and Politics in England in the 1930s* (1976).
John Hilton, *Rich Man, Poor Man* (1944).
A. Hutt, *The Condition of the Working Class in Britain* (1933).
John Lucas, *The 1930s: A Challenge to Orthodoxy* (1978).
Charles Loch Mowat, *Britain Between the Wars 1918–1940* (1955).
Malcolm Muggeridge, *The Thirties* (1940).
B. Seebohm Rowntree, *Poverty and Progress* (1941).
Stephen Spender, *The Thirties and After* (1978).
Margery Spring-Rice, *Working-Class Wives* (1939).
John Strachey, *The Coming Struggle for Power* (1932).
Julian Symons, *The Thirties: A Dream Revolved* (1975).
A.J.P. Taylor, *The Origins of the Second World War* (1961); *English History 1914–1945* (1965).
Hugh Thomas, *The Spanish Civil War* (1961).
A.T. Tolley, *The Poetry of the Thirties* (1975).
Ellen Wilkinson, *The Town that was Murdered* (1939).

One of the best ways of getting the 'feel' of the period is by browsing through the newspapers of the period (many libraries, for instance, have *The Times* and sometimes other leading newspapers on microfilm) or such magazines as *Picture Post* (excellent as a pictorial record) and *Punch* (strong on political satire).

Index